Manual of

Plate 1.

CHINESE PAINTED SILKS, 18TH CENTURY.

The Wordsworth
Manual
of Ornament

–

Richard Glazier

Wordsworth Reference

First published in Great Britain as *A Manual of Historic Ornament*, 1899.

This edition published 1995 by Wordsworth Editions Ltd, Cumberland House, Crib Street, Ware, Hertfordshire SG12 9ET.

ISBN 1-85326-347-8

Printed and bound in Denmark by Nørhaven.

The paper in this book is produced from pure wood pulp, without the use of chlorine or any other substance harmful to the environment. The energy used in its production consists almost entirely of hydroelectricity and heat generated from waste materials, thereby conserving fossil fuels and contributing little to the greenhouse effect.

PREFACE.

This manual has been prepared with the three-fold object of giving an elementary knowledge of Architecture and Historic Ornament, of awakening a responsive and sympathetic feeling for the many beautiful and interesting remains of ancient and mediæval civilization, and lastly, of directing the attention of students and craftsmen to the beauty, suggestiveness, and vitality of the Industrial arts of the past, and their intimate relation to the social and religious life of the people.

The advantages to be derived by students and craftsmen from such a study are manifold, for, by a careful study of these arts we may see the capabilities and limitations of material, the appropriateness and application of ornament, the continuity of line and form—yet with a marked diversity of enrichment and treatment—the interest and significance of detail, and the customs, myths, and traditions of the past, with their range of thought and expression.

The illustrations, which have been chosen expressly for this work, are typical examples of each period or style, and are produced in line as being the method best suited to the requirements of students, giving definition, emphasis, and constructive qualities of design rather than pictorial effect.

In the appendix will be found a list of text-books and works of reference, which may be studied with considerable advantage by students desiring further information upon this important subject.

RICHARD GLAZIER.

MANCHESTER,
1899.

PUBLISHER'S NOTE

The plates in this book have been arranged in such a way that, as far as possible, the illustrations face the relevant descriptive text for the convenience of the reader. This has inevitably resulted in the occurrence of some right-hand blank pages.

CONTENTS.

ALPHABETICAL LIST OF PLATES.

ALPHABETICAL LIST OF PLATES—*cont.*

ILLUSTRATIONS IN THE TEXT.

Part I.
The History and Development of Architecture & Ornament.

1. Eskimo engraving on bone.
*2. Ornament with fish hawks, Solomon Islands.
*3. Basketwork hat, with whaling scene, N.W. America.
*4. Ornament derived from creeper shoots, Iban, Borneo.
5. Painted earthenware, Ica, Peru.
*6. Dragonfly diaper, Bushongo pipe, Congo.
7. Bird ornament, textile, Pachacamac, Peru.
*8. Shale pipe, with totemic carvings, Queen Charlotte Islands.
9. Vase from Knossos, Crete.

British Museum Ethnographical Collection.

RIMITIVE ORNAMENT.

The ornament of primitive races presents a vast field for study, which it is difficult to focus adequately, and which has not yet been fully investigated. It is only possible here to note a few isolated instances. Some of its manifestations have a distinct degree of kinship to the scanty remains which have survived of the work of the long prehistoric eras, and also show similarities with departments of decorative art in such highly-developed yet self-contained civilisations as Crete and Peru. Examples of the work of these two latter styles are here included for comparison, Figs. 5, 7 and 9. The first patterns were probably the simple rows of roughly incised diagonal lines on early vessels, such as the beakers. Geometrical patterning on pottery naturally originates readily and spontaneously, and is found with a considerable degree of similarity in many parts of the world. These naturally develop after ages into chevrons, frets, scrolls and wave-like forms, which can be effectively combined, distributed and coloured, as in vases from Istria, and Cypriote work. One mask from Benin has interlacements markedly reminiscent of Celtic ornament. Geometrical design is used with much effectiveness by the Indians of the Americas, as in wampum beadwork, basketry, and blankets, and also in the leatherwork and palm-cloth of Central Africa. In metal and ceramic work of the Iron Age abstract design is found with naturalistic or conventional figures, which are used in panel or frieze form. But widely distant peoples have sometimes succeeded in the effective conventionalisation of animal and plant forms, as in a dragonfly diaper wood-carving on a Congo pipe (Fig. 6), and the hawk-ornament from the Solomon Islands (Fig. 2). The sea forms of Cretan pottery are vigorous if naturalistic. From Borneo comes some effective floral ornament derived from the shoots of a creeper (Fig. 4), and the Kenyak-Kayan tribes have mixed with the scrolls of their carved houseboards humanistic figures and dog-like forms. The Eskimo have graphically and ingeniously represented the activities of a whole settlement by engraving in narrow strips on ivory or bone (Fig. 1). The Indians of North-west America have inserted a version of a whale hunt on a hat of basketwork (Fig. 3), and like many other peoples, can turn the human face to account by varied repetition. The totem poles of British Columbia are crowded with figures and other devices, in a style which is applied to various objects, and often rises, as in a shale pipe of the Haida of Queen Charlotte Island, to a Breughel-like grotesqueness (Fig. 8). Tribal ornament ranges from a few casual scrappy patterns, like those of such peoples of low type as the aboriginal Australians, to vigorous pattern, well distributed, and carried out with feeling for the character of the material. The craftsman has generally made use of his chances, and produced achievements among races of widely differing culture and many periods all over the globe.

3

1

2

3

A HUMAN
FIGURE   ANCIENT PATAKA SLABS.
IN CARVED WOOD   AUCKLAND MUSEUM

OLD CARVED LINTEL
AUCKLAND MUSEUM.

4

CANOE STERNPOST. AUCKLAND MUSEUM. NEW ZEALAND

5

6

CARVED BOX NEW ZEALAND BRITISH MUSEUM.

7

8

PATAKA SLAB
AUCKLAND. M

BOX FOR FEATHERS NEW ZEALAND B.M.

CLUB
NEW
ZEA-
LAND

10
WOOD
MERE

11
WHALEBONE
COMB
NEW
ZEALAND.

12
KNIFE

NEW
ZEA-
LAND.

13
TER-
MINAL
HEAD OF
PADDLE
MANGAIA
HEAPE COLLECTION.

14
BOX
INCISED
ORNAMENT
SOLOMON
ISLAND.

15

HEAD
OF
PADDLE
MANGAIA

ORNAMENT OF OCEANIA.

The ornamentation of the people of the Pacific Isles is full of interest, and is remarkable for the evolution and perfecting of an ornamental style by a primitive people, with myths and traditions purely local, and in no way influenced by other nations. It is a style of ornament full of meaning and symbolism, yet simple in detail and arrangement, not founded upon the beautiful vegetation and flora of their islands, but upon abstract forms derived from the human figure, and arranged with a pleasing geometrical precision remarkable for a primitive people.

The ornamental art of these people may be broadly divided into provinces, each with its distinct ornamental characteristics and traditions, New Zealand showing the highest development and Australia the lowest in the ornament of Polynesia and Melanesia.

Much of the ornament is purely linear, consisting of parallel and zig-zag lines ; that of Australia consists almost entirely of these lines incised in the ground and occasionally filled in with colour. In New Guinea a higher development is reached, the ornament, of straight and curved lines, being carved in flat relief. In the province of Tonga-Samoa, the surface is

ORNAMENT FROM A CLUB. SAMOA.

NEW GUINEA SHIELD

divided into small fields, and the linear ornament runs in a different direction on each of the fields. The Hervey and Austral Islands are distinguished by their remarkable adaptations of the human female figure, the illustrations given here showing the original type and its ornamental development. These examples, together with the circular eye pattern, form the elements of the Hervey province, of which the Heape collection contains many fine examples. In the Solomon Island the

linear ornament is occasionally interspersed with an inlay of angular pieces of mother of pearl. The New Zealand province is distinguished by its skilful pieced carving, the beauty of its spiral forms adapted from the human figure (figs. 1-12), and the constant use of the border here given. No preliminary design was used, nor was the pattern outlined upon the object of the decoration. It was, so to speak, evolved from the artist's head as he worked, much as a musician improvises at the piano. This art, once general, now appears to be falling rapidly into oblivion.

5

WINGED GLOBE AND ASPS.

2

THE SCARABÆUS OR SACRED BEETLE.

HATHORIC
CAPITAL SUR-
MOUNTED BY A
NAOS· PHILÆ
B C
106.

3

4

5

COLUMNS FROM
THEBES B.C 1250.

6

RELIEF FROM THE BRITISH MUSEUM.

16

15

THE EGYPTIAN LOTUS.

7

8

9

10

EXAMPLES OF PAINTED
ORNAMENT. 1800 B.C.

GYPTIAN ORNAMENT.

The history of Egypt extends from nearly 4000 B.C. to 340 B.C.

The capitals of the Ancient Empire comprised Memphis and Abydos ; of the Middle Empire, Thebes, Luxor, and Tanis ; and of the New Empire, Sais and Bubastes. The remarkable civilization of these early dynasties is attested by the many fine remains of architecture, sculpture, and decorative arts that enrich our national museums. The three great periods of Egyptian art are *Memphite* (fourth, fifth, and sixth dynasties) in which figure sculpture appears somewhat heavy, but accurate ; the *Theban* Age (from the eleventh to the twenty-first dynasty) ; and the *Sait* or Neo-Memphite Age. The sculptures of the second Theban Empire are important and numerous.

The Sphinx, half animal and half human, is probably of the VI. dynasty, yet it is singular that all the earliest sculptures of the III. and IV. dynasties with which we are acquainted were realistic portraiture, remarkable for fidelity to nature. Kings, queens, and individuals of note were finely sculptured, frequently of a colossal size. But the Deities, Amen Sekhet, Horus, Hathor, Isis, and Osiris were represented in the later dynasties by small votive statuettes, noticeable for their number rather than for their artistic qualities, never reaching the excellence or vitality of the earlier period. Much of the architectural enrichment was in *Cavo Relievo*, a peculiarly Egyptian mode of ornamentation, the outline of the figures, birds, or flowers being sunk into the surface of the granite or basalt, and then carved within this sunk outline, leaving the ground or bed raised, these reliefs being invariably painted red, blue, green, and yellow. The frieze, which in the hands of the Greeks, at a later period, became their principal ornamental field, was used by the Egyptians in superposed bands, showing, in *cavo relievo*, the industrial arts and pursuits—weaving, glass blowing, and the making of pottery ; ploughing, sowing, and reaping ; also hunting and fishing. The composition and sculpture of these incidents was simple, refined, and purely decorative, with a *naïveté* and unaffectedness appropriate to the architectonic conditions. Mingled with these incidents were the beautiful hieroglyphs, or picture writing of the Egyptians. Figs. 7-13 are examples of painted decorations showing the spiral construction of lines, together with the symbolic treatment of the Lotus, the latter being regarded by the Egyptians as a symbol of fertility and of a new life, hence the profusion with which it was used in their decorative work. Great fertility of invention was displayed in enriching their architectural capitals with the Lotus, the Papyrus, and the Palm. A singular feature introduced during the XVIII. dynasty was the Hathor Capital, surmounted by a small Naos. During the Ptolemaic period—300 B.C.—the Hathor Capital was placed upon the vertical bell-shaped capital (fig. 3).

7

BAS-RELIEF.
BRITISH MUSEUM.
1

COLUMN
FROM
PERSE-
POLIS
4

2

3

ORNAMENT FROM NIMROUD

SCULPTURED PAVEMENT
FROM KOUJUNJIK
BRITISH MUSEUM.

7

5

6

AN ASSYRIAN
PATERA.

ORNAMENT FROM PERSEPOLIS.

8

BAS-RELIEF
IN ALABASTER
BRITISH
MUSEUM.

8

SSYRIAN ORNAMENT.

The early history of Babylonia and Assyria is one long series of wars and conquests. Originally one nation, they became divided, and the younger Assyria in the north became the most powerful empire of that period, under Tiglath-Phalasar I., 1100 B.C., Ashur-nasir-pal, 885-60 B.C., Shalmaneser II., 860-25 B.C., Tiglath-Phalasar III., 745-27 B.C., the Great Sargon, 722-705 B.C., Senna-cherib, 705-681 B.C., Esarhaddon, 681-668 B.C., and Ashur-ban-pal, 668-626 B.C. In 609 B.C. the capital, Nineveh, was destroyed by Cyaxares the Mede, and Babylon arose again to power under Nebuchadnezzar, 604-562 B.C. : this city was destroyed by Cyrus the Persian, 539 B.C.

Assyrian art, with its racial influences, religious beliefs, and climatic conditions, differs in a remarkable degree from Egyptian art. Though stone is found in Assyria, the great cities were built of brick, no doubt owing to the fact of the arts and civilization coming from Chaldea, where stone was scarce and clay plentiful. Both at Babylon in Chaldea and Nineveh in Assyria the traditional type of building was rectangular, with arched openings and vaults, built of sun-dried bricks. The lower part of the wall was covered with large alabaster slabs, carved in low relief with scenes representing the king and his warriors engaged in hunting or fighting (fig. 1). The upper part of the wall was in enamelled brick, or in coloured stucco, with details of the Lotus and the bud, together with the rosette, which was often carried round the archivolt. The representation of the industrial arts and the pursuits of agriculture, which is so admirably illustrated upon the Egyptian reliefs, is entirely absent in Assyria. The enamelled bricks of Chaldea were modelled in low relief, with enamels of turquoise blue, yellow, white, and black, of fine quality and colour—one splendid example of enamel on beton is the Frieze of Archers from the Palace of Susa (p. 19). The enamelled bricks of Assyria were usually flat, or modelled but slightly, and the enamels were less pure. The external walls were similar to the internal ones, but with larger friezes and bolder reliefs, and usually with religious subjects (fig. 9). The portals were enriched with colossal winged and human-headed bulls, of alabaster, finely carved in relief. Typical examples of Assyrian ornament are the Lotus and the bud (figs. 2 and 3), the Patera or Rosette (figs. 6 and 7), and the Hom, or Tree of Life (fig. 8). The Lotus enrichment shows Egyptian influence, and only came into use during the 7th century B.C., when intercourse between the two nations was estab-lished. It is differentiated from the Egyptian Lotus by its vigorous growth and curved profile, and the geometrical form of the calyx of the flower and bud (fig. 2).

The type of Anthemion or *Hom*, with its alternate bud and fir-cone, and with strong lateral markings, is beautiful in line and proportion of mass (fig. 3). The *Hom* is frequently used as a flower on the sacred tree, a form of enrichment that influenced much of the later Persian and Sicilian textile fabrics.

Height of columns, 11′ 7½″ or 20 modules.

CORINTHIAN ORDER. FROM THE MONUMENT OF LYSICRATES, ATHENS. B.C. 335.

Height of column 25 feet or 19 modules.

THE IONIC ORDER. THE ERECTHEUM, ATHENS.

DETAILS FROM THE GREEK IONIC ORDER.

OVOLO, FROM THE CORNICE.

CYMA REVERSA, FROM THE ARCHITRAVE.

ENRICHMENT FROM THE CAPITAL.

METOPE.

TRIGLYPH.

Height of column, 31′ 4″ or 10¼ modules.

THE DORIC ORDER. THE PARTHENON, ATHENS.

GREEK ARCHITECTURE.

Classic or columnar architecture is divided into the Greek and Roman styles, and each style comprises several orders of architecture: the Grecian orders are the Doric, the Ionic, and the Corinthian, and many examples of each of these orders are still extant in Greece and her colonies—Asia Minor, Southern Italy, and Sicily. From a comparison of these buildings, certain constructive and decorative features are observed to be present, and thence they are considered as the characteristics of the style or order, which comprises the Base (except in the Grecian Doric, which has no base), Column and Capital, and the Entablature, which consists of the Architrave, Frieze, and Cornice. The proportions of these orders are generally determined by the lower diameter of the column, which is divided into 2 modules or 60 parts, the height of the column always including the base and capital. The DORIC order was used for the early Greek temples from 650 B.C., and culminated in the Parthenon, 438 B.C. The COLUMNS in this order are 4½ to 6 diameters in height, with 20 shallow flutings with intermediate sharp arrises; the CAPITAL is half a diameter in height, and is composed of an echinus or ovolo moulding with annulets or deep channellings below, and a large square abacus above. The ARCHITRAVE is plain; the FRIEZE is enriched by rectangular blocks, with 3 vertical channellings in the face, termed triglyphs, alternately with square metopes which were frequently sculptured. The CORNICE, composed of simple mouldings, projects considerably beyond the face of the frieze.

CARYATIDE,
ERECHTHEUM.

The IONIC order has COLUMNS of from 9 to 9½ diameters in height, with 24 flutings divided by narrow fillets; the BASE is half a diameter in height, and composed of a plinth, torus, fillet, cavetto, fillet, torus, and fillet. The CAPITAL is $\frac{1}{10}$ of a diameter high, and consists of a pair of double scrolls or volutes, supported by an echinus moulding enriched with the egg and tongue, with an astragal below.

The ENTABLATURE is one quarter the height of the columns, the ARCHITRAVE of one or more fascias, the FRIEZE continuous and frequently enriched with sculpture in low relief; the CORNICE has simple and compound mouldings supported by a dentil band. Caryatides were occasionally introduced into this order; they were female figures clad in drapery having vertical folds which re-echoed the flutings of the Ionic column. These Caryatides supported the entablature in place of the columns; a beautiful example is in the south portico of the Erechtheum at Athens.

The CORINTHIAN order was not much used by the Greeks ; the examples, however, show considerable refinement and delicacy of details. The COLUMNS are 10 diameters in height, with 24 flutings ; the BASE is half a diameter high ; the CAPITAL is a little greater than a diameter in height, and is enriched with acanthus foliated leaves and spiral volutes. The ENTABLATURE is richer and the CORNICE deeper and more elaborate than those of the other orders.

The principal Doric buildings in Greece are :—The Temples at Corinth[2, 8], 650 B.C., Ægina[2, 8], 550 B.C., the Parthenon[2, 9], and the Theseum[2, 8], 438 B.C. ; the Temples of Jupiter at Olympia[2, 8], 436 B.C., Apollo Epicurius at Bassæ[2, 8], 430 B.C., Propylæa at Athens, 431, B.C. and the Minerva at Sunium, 420 B.C.   Ionic buildings are :—Temples at Ilyssus[1, 7], 484 B.C., Nike Apteros[1, 7], 420 B.C., and the Erechtheum, ca. 420 B.C. (see plan, plate 85), North Portico[7], East Portico[8], at Athens. In Asia Minor there are the Temples of Samos[8], Priene[8], Teos[8], Diana at Ephesus[9] (with 36 of its columns sculptured), and of Apollo at Miletos.   Corinthian buildings are :—The Monument of Lysicrates, 335 B.C., the Tower of the Winds (octagonal in plan), and Jupiter Olympius[2, 8], 200 B.C..

During the 5th century B.C. the Doric order was extensively used in the Greek colonies at Sicily.   At Agrigentum there are the remains of six fine Doric temples, of which the Temple of Zeus[2], 450 B.C., is the largest, being 354 by 175 feet.   In this Temple were found the *Telemones*, or *Atlantes*, male figures, 25 feet in height, with their arms raised, probably supporting the roof.   This Temple is also remarkable for its portico of seven columns, 60 feet in height, and having the peristyle walled up.

At Selinus there are five large Doric temples[2, 8], and one[5, 9] with columns 57 feet in height, with an entablature of 19 feet.   At Segesta there is a Doric temple[2, 8] with only the peristyle complete and the columns unfluted, and at Pæstum, in Southern Italy, there are two Doric temples[2, 8] and a basilica[5] with its porticos of nine columns each.

All these buildings in Sicily and Pæstum date between 500 and 430 B.C.

CLASSIFICATION OF CLASSIC TEMPLES.

ARRANGEMENT OF COLUMNS AND WALLS.

[1] *Apteral* - When the side walls have no colonnade.
[2] *Peripteral* - When there is a colonnade standing apart from the side walls.
[3] *Pseudo-peripteral* When the colonnade is attached to the side walls.
[4] *Dipteral* - When there is a double colonnade standing out from the walls.
[5] *Pseudo-dipteral* - When the inner row of columns is attached to the side walls.

THE RELATION OF THE ENDS OF THE TEMPLE.

In Antis - - When the columns do not project beyond the ends of the side walls.
Prostyle - When a portico stands in front of the temple.
[6] *Amphi-prostyle* - When there is a portico at each end.
Mono-prostyle - If the portico is one column in depth.
Di-prostyle - If the portico is two columns in depth.

THE NUMBER OF COLUMNS IN THE PORTICO.

[7] *Tetrastyle* - - If of four columns.
[8] *Hexastyle* - - If of six columns.
[9] *Octastyle* - - If of eight columns.

MONUMENT of
LYSICRATES.
ATHENS. B.C. 335.

PROPORTIONS OF THE ENTABLATURE, IN PARTS.

		Archi-trave.	Frieze.	Cornice.	Total Entablature.
Doric -	Parthenon -	44½	40½	26	111
	Theseus -	50	55½	25½	131
Ionic -	Erechtheum	51½	48½	37½	137½
	Priene -	46½	29	55⅝	131½
Corinthian	Lysicrates -	51	39½	50	140½
	Jupiter Olympius	41⅝	27½	48	117

IONIC ORDER, TEMPLE OF
ILYSSUS.

ANTHEMION ORNAMENT.
FROM GREEK
TOMBS.

3 FEET

SIDE
ELEVATION
OF CONSOLE.
A

1' 7"

DETAIL OF THE
ARCHITRAVE OF
NORTH DOOR.
ERECHTHEUM.
ATHENS.

SIZE OF
OPENING.
HEIGHT 16'. 8"
WIDTH.(Lower diameter 7'.10"
—— Upper · 7'.4"

14

REEK ORNAMENT.

Greece, or Hellas, consisted of a number of small states, speaking the same language, and worshipping the same gods. Almost the whole of the Ægean coast of Asia Minor was occupied in early times by Greek Colonies, which supplanted those of the Phœnicians of Tyre and Sidon. The southern portion of this seaboard was occupied by the Dorians, and the northern by Ionians. In the course of time other Greek settlements were made on the Black Sea and Mediterranean Coast of Asia Minor, as well as at Syracuse, Gela and Agrigentum in Sicily, and in Etruria and Magna Grecia in Italy. These colonies appear to have reached a higher state of art at an earlier period than Greece itself. The ascendancy in art in Greece was enjoyed by the Dorians circa 800 B.C.; after which Sparta took the lead but was in turn excelled by the Ionians, when Athens became the focus of Greek art, and attained a degree of perfection in that respect that has remained unequalled to this day. Athens was destroyed by the Persians under Xerxes, 480 B.C.; but under Pericles (470-429 B.C.) Greek art reached its culmination.

The abundant, although fragmentary, remains of Grecian architecture, sculpture, and the industrial arts show most vividly the artistic feeling and culture of the early Greeks, with their great personality and religious sentiment, in which the personal interest of the gods and goddesses was brought into relation with the life and customs of the people. Their myths and traditions, their worship of legendary heroes, the perfection of their physical nature, and their intense love of the beautiful, were characteristic of the Greek people, from the siege of Troy to their subjection by Rome, 140 B.C. The almost inexhaustible store of Greek art, now gathered in the British and in other European museums, furnishes one of the most valuable illustrations of the many glorious traditions of the past. The vitality of conception, the dignity and noble grace of the gods, the consummate knowledge of the human figure, and the exquisite skill of craftsmanship, are here seen in the greatest diversity of treatment and incident.

The work of Phidias, the most renowned of Greek sculptors, is largely represented in the British Museum by noble examples, showing his great personality, wonderful power, and his remarkable influence upon contemporary and later plastic art.

The Parthenon, or temple of the goddess Athene (plan, plate 85), which was built upon the Acropolis at Athens by Ictinus and Callicrates, 454-438 B.C., was enriched with splendid works of sculpture by Phidias. Many of the originals are now in the British Museum forming part of the Elgin Marbles, which were purchased from the Earl of Elgin in 1815. The two pediments of the temple contained figure sculpture in the round, larger than life size. The Eastern group represents the birth of Athene, and the western group the contest of Athene and Poseidon

15

ELEVATION OF THE
PARTHENON.
ATHENS.

WIDTH 101 FEET

for the soil of Attica. The fragments of these pedimental groups are now in the British Museum, and, though sadly mutilated, show the perfection of sculpture during the Phidian age. Of the 92 square metopes sculptured in high relief that enriched the Doric frieze, 15 are included in the Elgin Marbles. The subject represented on these metopes was the battle between the Centaurs and Lapithæ—a fine example of composition of line and mass, and dramatic power of expression.

DORIC FRIEZE. FROM THE PARTHENON. ATHENS.

The continuous frieze upon the upper part of the cella wall, under the colonnade or Peristyle, was 40 feet from the ground, 40 inches in height, and 523 feet in length. It was carved in low relief, the subject being the Panathenæic procession, the most sacred and splendid of the religious festivals of the Ancient Greeks. This frieze, with its rhythm of movement and unity of composition, its groups of beautiful youths and maidens, sons and daughters of noble citizens, its hero-

16

and deities, heralds and magistrates; its sacrificial oxen, and its horses and riders is doubtless a most perfect production of the sculptors' art. Each figure is full of life and motion, admirable in detail, having an individuality of action and expression, yet with a unity of composition, appropriate to its architectural purpose as a frieze or band.

The Parthenon, however, was but the shrine of the standing figure or statue of the goddess Athene, which was 37 feet high, and formed of plates of gold and ivory, termed *Chryselephantine* sculpture. Probably owing to the intrinsic value of the material, this work of Phidias disappeared at an early date.

Among the examples of sculptured marbles in the British Museum is the beautiful frieze from the interior of the Temple of Apollo at Bassæ or Phigaleia erected by Ictinus, 430 B.C. This frieze, which shows an extraordinary vitality and movement, is 101 feet long and consists of 23 slabs 25½ inches in width, the incidents depicted being the battle of the Greeks and the Amazons, and the contest between the Centaurs and the Lapithæ. The dignity and reserve of the Parthenon frieze is here replaced by activity and energy of line and an exuberance of modelling.

Some of the marbles in the British Museum are from the Nereid Monument of Xanthos, 372 B.C., so called because the female figures display moist clinging garments, and have fishes and seabirds between their feet. These sculptures show a high degree of perfection, and were probably the work of the Athenian sculptor, Bryaxis.

Among other examples of the Greek treatment of the frieze, is that of the Erechtheum, 409 B.C., with its black Eleusinian stone background, and white marble reliefs. The Temple of Nike Apteros, of about the same date, is noted for the beautiful reliefs from the balustrade which crowned the lofty bastion on which the temple stands. An example of Nike or victory, adjusting her sandal is here given. These reliefs are remarkable for their delicacy and refinement of treatment, and the exquisite rendering of the draped female figure. Other friezes now in the British Museum are from the Mausoleum erected by Artemisia to her husband, Mausolus, 357-348 B.C. This tomb consisted of a solid basement of masonry, supporting a cella surrounded by a colonnade of 36 columns. The upper part of the basement was enriched with a frieze illustrating the battle of the Centaurs and Lapithæ; the frieze of the cella was illustrated with funeral games in honour of Mausolus. Seventeen slabs of the frieze of the order from the colonnade are in the British Museum; they represent the battle of the Greeks and Amazons.

BAS-RELIEF, FROM NIKE APTEROS.

In their composition these slabs show extraordinary energy of movement and richness of invention. This frieze differs absolutely from the Parthenon frieze in its fertility of incident and intensity of action Bryaxis, the sculptor of the Nereid monument executed the north frieze, while the south was by Timotheus, the east by Scopas, and the west by Leochares.

A remarkable building, where again the frieze was an important feature, was the great altar at Pergamos, erected by Eumenes II., 168 B.C. This had a basement of masonry 160 feet by 160 feet, and 16 feet high, enriched with a sculptured frieze 7½ feet high. The subject is the *Gigantomachia*, or battle of the gods and giants; the treatment being characterized by passionate energy and expression, and daring skill in grouping and technique. Ninety-four of the original slabs of this frieze are now in the Berlin Museum.

The frieze was an important decorative feature with the Assyrians and Greeks. The continuity of incident and rhythm of movement that was possible with the continuous frieze, together with its functional use of banding, no doubt tended to preserve its traditional form, hence we have many remains from antiquity of this beautiful decorative treatment. An early and fine example is the frieze of Archers from the palace of Susa, 485 B.C., now in Louvre. This frieze,

18

of which an illustration is here given, was executed in enamel on beton. A dignity of conception and unity of composition were here combined with skilful modelling of relief work, and fine colouring of blue, turquoise and yellow. This treatment of the frieze no doubt influenced the later work of the Greeks, who so nobly carried on this tradition of the frieze.

Greek ornament is distinguished by simplicity of line, refinement of detail, radiation of parts, unity of composition, and perfect symmetry. The anthemion, which is the typical form, differs from the earlier Lotus type in its more abstract rendering and its absence of symbolism; it has a charm of composition and a unity and balance of parts.

FRIEZE IN ENAMELLED BRICKS FROM THE PALACE OF SUSA 485 B.C. LOUVRE

The anthemion was sculptured upon the top of the funeral stele (figs. 1, 2, and 5, plate 8), upon the architrave of doorways (fig. 6), and above the necking of the Ionic columns (plate 6), or painted upon the panels of the deep coffered ceilings. It was also used in a thousand ways upon the many fine vases and other ceramic wares of that period. The simplicity and beauty of the anthemion and its ready adaptability, has doubtless rendered it one of the best known types of ornament. Like the Egyptian and Assyrian prototypes the Greek anthemion is usually arranged with alternate flower and bud, connected by a curved line or more frequently by a double spiral. Illustrations are given on plates 8 and 9 of a few typical examples, where the rhythm and beauty of composition are indicative of the culture and perfection of Greek craftsmanship.

Another feature, which at a later period received considerable development, was the scroll given on plate 9, which is a fine example from the roof of the monument to Lysicrates. The scrolls, cut with V-shaped sections, spring from a nest of sharp acanthus foliage. This

EXAMPLES OF BANDS FROM GREEK VASES   OWEN JONES.

FROM THE MUSEUM   NAPLES

ORNAMENT IN MARBLE, FROM THE ROOF APEX, MONUMENT
OF LYSICRATES   ATHENS B.C. 335

scroll is formed of a series of spirals springing from each other, the junction of the spiral being covered by a sheath or flower ; the spiral itself being often broken by a similar sheath.

This spiral form, with its sheathing, is the basis of the Roman and Italian Renascence styles, and sharply differentiates them from the Gothic ornament, in which the construction line is continuous and unbroken.

The rosette, a survival of the early Greek form, found at Crete, (1600 B.C.) was frequently used upon the funeral stele and the Architrave (plate 8) where its circular and radiating form contrasts beautifully with the functional straight lines of architectural design. The extraordinary vitality and versatility of the Greek craftsman may be traced through a magnificent series of coins dating from 700 B.C. to 280 B.C. The interest of subject, beauty of composition and largeness of style, combined with the utmost delicacy of technique, of these gold, silver, and electrum coins, are a reflex of the artistic feeling for beauty of the early Greeks.

Colour, as well as form, was a great factor in the art of the Greeks ; their architecture and sculpture were enriched and accentuated by the judicious use of beautiful colour. The Parthenon, with its simple and refined Doric architecture and magnificent sculpture by Phidias, was enhanced by colour, which was introduced in the background of the pediment and the frieze, and also upon the borders and accessories of the draperies. The " Lacunaria," or sunk panels of the ceilings, were frequently enhanced with blue, having rosettes or stars in gold or colour. A frank use of pure colour was almost universal in early Egyptian and Assyrian art, and the Greeks were not slow to avail themselves of any art that was beautiful.

GREEK VASE OF THE STYLE OF NICOSTHENES (v. p. 107).

COIN OF PHILIP II B.C. 339-336.

COIN OF TERINA B.C 412.

COIN OF AGRIGENTUM B.C 412-406

HEIGHT OF COLUMNS. 38' 10".
OR 19 MODULES. 16 PARTS.

THE CORINTHIAN ORDER, FROM THE PORTICO OF THE PANTHEON, ROME.

HEIGHT OF COLUMNS. 29' 5'.
OR 20 MODULES. 6 PARTS

THE COMPOSITE ORDER, ARCH OF TITUS, ROME.

A MODILLION.

CYMA REVERSA.

THE IONIC ORDER, TEMPLE OF FORTUNA VIRILIS, ROME.

HEIGHT OF COLUMNS. 21' 11".
OR 17 MODULES. 12 PARTS.

ROMAN ARCHITECTURE.

Is differentiated from that of Greece by the extensive use of the arch and of superposed orders. The many fine remains of Roman temples and public buildings show the extraordinary versatility and conception of the Roman architects, their constructive skill, and their remarkable power of assimilating the arts of other nations. The Roman temples were somewhat similar in plan to their Greek prototypes, but usually without the side colonnade, larger in scale, and with an ostentatious display of mouldings and ornaments, less refined in contour and detail.

ARCH OF
SEPTIMIUS
SEVERUS
AT ROME

A typical example is given here of a triumphal arch, namely, that of Septimus Severus, A.D. 203. Other examples are the Arch of Titus, A.D. 81, and the Arch of Constantine, A.D. 326, all near the Forum at Rome. Trajan's Arch, A.D. 114, was destroyed by Constantine, who used many of the reliefs for the building of his own arch.

The superposition of columns and arches is seen in the Theatre of Marcellus, 20 B.C., where the lower order is of the Doric and the upper of the Ionic; this, like the early Greek Theatre, was semi-circular in plan.

The Colosseum, commenced by Vespasian, A.D. 72, and completed by

23

Domitian, A.D. 82, has a third storey, having the Corinthian order, and an attic storey with Corinthian pilasters, the whole reaching to a height of 157 feet. The diameters of the amphitheatre were 584 by 468 ft.

One of the best preserved buildings of the early Roman period is the Pantheon (plan, plate 85), built during the reign of Hadrian, A.D. 117-38. This has a fine dome of coffered panels, having a diameter of 142 ft., and an altitude of 71 ft. 6 in., with a total height of 143 ft. from the floor to eye of dome.

The beautiful octastyle Corinthian portico, of the time of Agrippa, 27 B.C., has granite columns 46 ft. 6 in. in height, with fine capitals in white marble.

The magnificent temple of Castor and Pollux, frequently called Jupiter Stator, is only known from the three columns still standing ; but these show the magnitude of scale and the exuberance of detail that characterized the finest period of Roman architecture. The proportions of this order are columns, 45 ft. 3 in. in height and the entablature 11 ft. 7 in.

The Tuscan and Composite orders were added to the Doric, Ionic, and Corinthian orders, thus forming the five orders of architecture.

The Romans rarely used the peristyle temple, consequently the cella was of the same width as the portico. In the civic buildings and palaces, the Romans show the greatest constructive skill

THE CORINTHIAN ORDER
FROM THE PANTHEON.

24

and splendour of embellishment. The skilful planning and appropriateness of decorative treatment in their basilicas and amphitheatres are evidences of the practical nature of the Romans.

The Basilica or Hall of Justice was an important architectural feature, rectangular in plan, with a semi-circular apse at one end, where the tribunal was placed ; roofed with timber framing, or vaulted with concrete, and supported with rows of columns or piers. The remains of two typical Roman basilicas are still in existence : the Basilica of Trajan, A.D. 114, rectangular, 180 by 160 ft., five aisles, the centre aisle with a semi-circular wooden roof, and enriched with bronze plates, is typical of one class ; and the Basilica of Maxentius, A.D. 310, with a width of 195 ft., and a length of 260 ft., is typical of a vaulted Basilica, the two side aisles with barrel-vaults, and the centre aisle with an intersecting vaulted roof.

The form of these Roman basilicas was adapted by the early Christians to their service, and the basilica church became the typical form used up to the 12th century in the former Roman provinces.

The Roman houses were of two types : the *Domus*, or houses clustered together, and the *Insular*, houses which were surrounded by streets. Most of the finest Pompeian houses were of the *Insular* type.

The usual plan of a Roman house consisted of the *Ostium*, an entrance or *Vestibule*, which opened into the *Atrium*, a large room or court partly roofed over, with an opening in the centre called the *Compluvium*, under which was the *Impluvium*, or cistern of water, placed below the level of the ground. Small chambers surrounded the *Atrium*, and at the further end was the *Tablinum* or private room, frequently leading to the *Peristylium* or private part of the house, an open court, with a colonnade surrounding a marble fountain, with flowers, shrubs, and trees, forming a *Viridarium*. Surrounding the *Peristylium* were private rooms, one of which was the *Triclinium*, or dining room. From the *Peristylium*, *fauces* or passages led to the *Porticus*, a colonnade which overlooked the garden.

25

FIG 1

42 INCHES

FRIEZE. FORUM OF TRAJAN. LATERAN MUSEUM.

2

3

26 INCHES

15 INCHES

ONE SIDE OF A SQUARE
SEPULCHRAL CIPPUS

ROMAN SCROLL

4 & 5
MARBLE
PANELS
BRITISH
MUSEUM·

14½

14½

6

PANEL OF VOTIVE CIPPIUS

8

7

32 INCHES

38 INCHES

TRIANGULAR BASE OF A MARBLE
CANDELABRUM. BRITISH MUSEUM.

FRIEZE. FORUM OF TRAJAN. ROME. 110 AD

26

ROMAN ORNAMENT.

Rome became, by successive wars and conquests, the mistress of the world, absorbing successively the arts and the architecture of the Etruscans, the Samnites, and of Corinth and Carthage. From these varied sources arose the style termed Roman, assimilating and adopting the column and the horizontal entablature of the Greeks ; the arch, the vault, the mural paintings, and the decorative use of bronze and terra-cotta of the Etruscans, with the sculpture, ornament, mosaics and coinage of the Greeks and Carthaginians. These varied arts were assimilated and perfected by the Romans during the period 100 B.C. to A.D. 337.

Roman ornament is the continuity of the Greek and Etruscan styles, consisting of the acanthus, the scroll and the anthemion ; the Romans using these forms with greater exuberance and elaboration, together with bold and vigorous carving, yet lacking the simplicity, refinement, and graceful contour of the Greek and Etruscan forms.

Roman ornament consists largely of continuous spiral lines, clothed with cups and sheaths of acanthus foliage, the various spirals terminating in a rosette. These main spirals are frequently interwoven with fine curved or spiral lines, clothed with acanthus or other foliation, such as the vine, olive, and ivy. Birds and reptiles and cupids, and the chimera or griffin (fig. 1) are often interspersed with the ornament, thus giving that largeness of mass, and contrast of form, which is so characteristic of Roman art. The Thermæ or baths, and public buildings, displayed decorative ceilings, having deep sunk panels called Lacunaria, or coffers ; square, hexagonal or octagonal in form, with a centre rosette in high relief and the border mouldings of the coffers being enriched with the egg and dart, or the water leaf.

COFFERED CEILING, BASILICA
OF MAXENTIUS.

These exhibit an effective treatment of moulded surfaces. The ceilings of the tombs and palaces were in many cases ornamented with circular

27

FIG. 1

3

MARBLE RELIEF IN THE UFFIZI GALLERY. FLORENCE

STUCCO DECORATION IN LOW RELIEF. REPRESENTING NYMPHS RIDING ON WINGED & SEA MONSTERS & NEREIDS SURROUNDED WITH ORNAMENT. FROM A TOMB ON THE VIA LATINA ROME. A.D. 160. DISCOVERED IN 1860. THE CEILING IS BARREL-VAULTED & ORNAMENTED. SEE FIG. 2.

2

STUCCO ORNAMENT IN LOW RELIEF UPON A CEILING IN TOMB VIA LATINA. ROME.

4

5

RELIEF PANEL FROM THE INSIDE OF THE PORTICO OF THE PANTHEON. ROME. A.D. 125.

6

CINERARY URN. BRITISH MUSEUM.

MARBLE URN. BRITISH MUSEUM.

and square panels, richly decorated with arabesques or mythical figures, and cupids in low relief of fine stucco ; the mouldings or divisions in higher relief, and having the water leaf or the egg and dart enrichment (plate 12).

The architectural frieze and the sepulchral urn and sarcophagi of this period were often decorated with festoons (figs. 4 and 5, plate 12), which were supported by cupids or by candelabra (plate 12), or by the skulls of oxen, as on the frieze from the Temple of Vesta at Tivoli, here given.

TEMPLE OF VESTA TIVOLI FRIEZE

The architectural basilica and forum of Trajan, erected A.D. 114, by Apollodorus, a Greek of Damascus, was of the utmost magnificence, the remains attesting to the skill and artistic craftsmanship of the Romans. Apollodorus also erected the marble column of Trajan, having a rectangular pedestal 18 ft. high, and richly sculptured with the dresses, armour and standards of the Roman army. This pedestal supports a column of the Tuscan order of architecture 97¼ ft. high, and 12ᶜ ft. in diameter, enriched with a series of spiral bands, having bas-reliefs representing the successive events of the Dacian War by the Emperor Trajan. This magnificent and well preserved relic of antiquity furnishes a complete epitome of the costumes and the arms and armour of that period. Another well preserved column, similar to that of Trajan, was erected in Rome by Marcus Aurelius, A.D. 174, the subjects of its reliefs being the war with the Marcomans. Large marble urns, or tazze, enriched with Bacchanalian figures, surrounded with foliage and birds and animals ; magnificent tables, chairs, couches, and candelabra, of bronze, enriched with silver damascening, together with the choice remains of sculpture and mosaics, all indicate the luxuriousness and love of magnificence of the wealthy Roman citizens.

In Roman architectural ornament we see the most powerful modelling combined with the use of the continuous scroll growing from a nest of foliage, repeated in their painted decorations (see Pompeian). This elaboration of typical ornamentation shows the rounded serrations of the Acanthus (see plate 11) and forms the chief characteristic of Roman ornament, which is wonderfully bold and vigorous in conception and execution, but deficient in the refinement and delicacy of Greek art.

There is a considerable difference in the foliations of the various capitals. The Corinthian capital of the Parthenon has foliage of the simple olive leaf type. In the composite capital of the Arch of Septimus Severus the foliage is serrated like fig. 8, plate 11, while that of the Corinthian capital of the Temple of Vesta, Tivoli, is more of the parsley leaf type, and each leaf is folded forward at the terminations.

FRIEZE FROM THE TEMPLE OF ISIS.

RED GROUND

A PAINTED PILLAR.

WALL DECORATION IN THE CASA DEL LABIRINTO. POMPEII.

PAINTED PILASTER FROM POMPEII. ZAHN'S POMPEII.

WALL DECORATION. FORUM OF HERCULES. POMPEII 79. A.D.

30

POMPEIAN ORNAMENT.

Pompeii, Herculaneum and Stabia, Roman cities, were buried by an eruption of Vesuvius, A.D. 79. These cities had already suffered from an earthquake, A.D. 63, and were being rapidly rebuilt when they were finally destroyed by the eruption. The Younger Pliny, the historian, was a spectator of the event at Pompeii, and wrote two letters to his friend Tacitus, describing the event and his flight from the doomed city, which remained buried for seventeen centuries, with the treasures of gold and silver, bronzes of rare workmanship, mural paintings on a most magnificent scale, and floors of mosaics of marvellous execution and design ; everything affording a vivid glimpse of the domestic and public life of the Romans of the 1st century A.D. Herculaneum was discovered in 1709, and Pompeii 1748, and from these cities many valuable remains of art have been taken. In the museum at Naples there are over 1,000 mural paintings, some 13,000 small bronzes, over 150 large bronzes of figures and busts, and 70 fine large mosaics.

A plan of a Roman house is given on page 25 showing the arrangement and use of the rooms. The floors were covered with mosaics (see plate 54), those of the vestibule, corridors, and small rooms having simple patterns enclosed with borders of the key pattern, or the guilloche in black, red, grey, and white tesseræ. The floor of the triclinium, or dining-room, was often a magnificent mosaic representing some mythological or classical subject. The walls were painted in colour, usually with a dado one-sixth the height of the wall, with pilasters dividing the wall into rectangular panels and a frieze above (plate 13). The general scheme of colour was, the dado and pilasters black, the panels red, and the frieze white ; or black dado, red pilasters and frieze, with white or yellow panels. The decoration upon these various coloured grounds was light and fanciful, and painted with great delicacy. Representations of architectural forms, such as columns and entablatures, are often rendered in perspective upon the painted walls.

The painted ornament has somewhat the same characteristics as the Roman relief work, but is usually much more delicate in treatment. The spiral form and the sheath are always prevalent, and from these sheaths and cups grow the finer tendrils or delicately painted spray of foliage, upon which birds are placed.

Stucco enrichments, such as ornamental string courses and mouldings, were frequently combined with the painted ornament ; they consist of small details, such as the water leaf, the egg and dart, and the anthemion, and are repeated in a regular series.

Herculaneum differed considerably from Pompeii, for here the finest works of art and innumerable MSS. have been found, showing that a higher intellectual life existed than that at Pompeii, where not a single MS. has been found.

FROM
ST MARKS
VENICE.

LILY
CAPITAL.
ST MARKS.

CAPITAL
FROM SAN
VITALE
RAVENNA

PIERCED
MARBLE
SCREEN.
ST MARKS.

SARCOPHAGI OF THEODSIUS 7TH CENTURY. S. APOLLINARE. RAVENNA.

PIERCED MARBLE
SCREEN. ST MARKS.

FROM ST MARKS.

CARVED PANELS IN ALABASTER FROM ST MARKS. VENICE. 1071.

ANCIENT
PIER.
VENICE.

CAPITAL. SANTA SOPHIA,
CONSTANTINOPLE.

"WINDBLOWN" CAPITAL. ST. MARK'S,
VENICE.

SCULPTURED FRIEZE. SARCOPHAGUS OF THE ARCHBISHOP THEODORE, RAVENNA.

SCULPTURED SLAB TORCELLO.

BYZANTINE ORNAMENT.

The decline of the Roman empire, in the 3rd and 4th centuries A.D., had its inevitable influence upon contemporary art, but perhaps a more potent influence was that of Christianity, which, in the reign of Constantine, received State recognition and support; and when this Emperor removed the seat of government from Rome to Byzantium, the traditional Greek and Roman arts were assimilated with those of Persia and Syria, but moulded and influenced by the new religion, giving that strong vitality, deep significance, and symbolism which is so remarkable a feature of the Byzantine style.

The change of style did not take place immediately, for most of the buildings erected by Constantine were in the traditional Roman style, but the arts were gradually perfected until they culminated in the building of S. Sophia, by Anthemius of Tralles and Isidorus of Miletus, during the reign of Justinian, A.D. 538. This building is remarkable for its splendid dome, supported by semi-domes and pendentives on a square plan (see plate 85), its embellishment with mosaics of glorious colours, and the great inventiveness and symbolism of the detail. The traditional sharp acanthus foliage of the Greeks was united with the emblems of Christianity, such as the circle, the cross, the vine, and the dove ; the peacock also is frequently seen. Figure sculpture was rarely used, but groups of figures were used in great profusion in the gold-ground mosaics that covered the upper part of the walls and the vaults and domes of the magnificent Byzantine buildings. The churches of Ravenna, in Italy, have somewhat similar characteristics : S. Vitale, A.D. 535, the basilica churches of S. Apollinare Nuovo, A.D. 493-525, S. Apollinare in Classe, A.D. 535-45, together with the Baptisteries, are rich in mosaics and sculptured capitals of the 6th and 7th centuries. In the cathedrals of Torcello, A.D. 670, and Murano, and the beautiful S. Mark's at Venice, marbles and mosaics were used in great profusion to enhance the architecture. The sketch plans given on plate 85 are typical of Byzantine planning, in which the symbolism of the circle and cross are used as constructive features. This symbolism is a marked feature in Byzantine ornament ; interlacing circles and crosses mingle with the acanthus or the vine, and are cut with a peculiar V-shaped section. The circular drill is largely used at the sinking of the leaves, and but little of the background is visible in the sculptured ornament of this period.

Pierced marble screens of interlaced foliage, or the fret in combination with their circle, were frequently used (see plate 84). A large number of pierced parapets in S. Mark's are carved in low relief, with various modifications of the interlacing guilloche, or circles.

33

FRIEZE FROM THE CHURCH OF SAINT-GILLES. PROVENCE.

PORTION OF ENGLISH MS. A D 1020. BRITISH MUSEUM.

DETAIL FROM DOORWAY. S² AGOSTINA.

CAPITAL FROM LAON

BASE OF COLUMNS MODENA CATHEDRAL.

BASE OF COLUMNS. WEST DOOR VERONA CATHEDRAL

PORTAL FROM SAINT-GILLES, PROVENCE

ROMANESQUE ARCHITECTURE & ORNAMENT.

Romanesque architecture is characterized chiefly by the universal use of the arch, the absence of the classic entablature, and in the imagery and symbolism of its sculpture and ornament, doubtless due to Northern influence. One of the earliest existing buildings of this style is the church of S. Ambrogio, Milan (11th century), which has a nave and aisles, three eastern apses, and a western atrium, surrounded by an open arcade, enriched with vigorous reliefs of interlaced ornament and animals. Contemporary in date is S. Michele, Pavia, with a nave and transepts and central cupola : there is a single eastern apse, having an open external gallery and bands of sculptured ornament. This and the frequent use of the lion or griffin as a support for pillars, are characteristic of the Lombardic style, and are seen at S. Michele, Lucca, and the Cathedral, Baptistery, and the Campanile of Pisa, and the Cathedral at Trogir, Dalmatia.

It was, however, in France and Germany that the Romanesque reached its highest development, principally in the south and south-west of France, where the churches are distinguished for the richness of the west fronts.

S. Trophime, Arles (12th century), has a fine low semi-circular projecting porch, resting upon a sculptured frieze and pillars. A cloister, with arcading of coupled columns richly sculptured, is attached to this church ; while S. Gilles (1076) has a low projecting porch of three arches, enriched with vigorous sculpture and ornament (plate 16).

The Cathedral at Angoulême has a vaulted nave, with three cupolas, and a west front with recessed arcading and figures : two square towers, with open arcading and conical spires, rise from the angles of the façade. Notre Dame, Poitiers, is even more rich in its gabled west front, having a fine doorway with two tiers of arcading above. The façade is flanked by two circular turrets, with massive columns attached, having an open arcade above, with a conical spire ; enriched corbel tables are carried across the front, over the door, the upper arcade and window, and round the turrets.

Saint-Front, Périgueux, has a richly sculptured west front and nave of the 11th century, to which was added, in 1150, a larger church similar in plan to S. Mark's at Venice (a Greek cross, see plate 85), and roofed with five cupolas in stone. In central France there was the magnificent Abbey Church of Cluny, with its range of six towers ; and in Germany this number of towers is found at the great Romanesque churches of Speyer, Worms, and Laach, with their singular western apse and external clearstory gallery.

Plate 16 illustrates a few of the chief features of Romanesque ornament. The upper frieze is similar to the Roman scroll, but less vigorous in modelling, and with a rounder form of serration of leaf form. The Laon capital has rich interlacing ornament and animals that suggest Scandinavian influence. The portal of Saint-Gilles shows the exuberant carving and storiation that characterized many of the churches of south-west France.

A CELTIC
INITIAL
1

2
INITIAL
FROM THE GOSPELS OF
LINDISFARNE
END OF 7TH CENTURY
BRITISH MUSEUM.

CELTIC INTERLACEING FRET
3

4
INTERLACED ANIMALS. FROM THE BOOK
OF KELLS. 8TH CENTY. BRITISH MUSEUM

5
CAREW CROSS.

6 BRONZE
SHIELD ENRICHED WITH RED
ENAMELS. BRITISH MUSEUM.

7
PORTION OF THE
TRUMPET PATTERN
OR DIVERGENT
SPIRAL. FROM
THE BOOK OF
DURROW. TRINITY COLLEGE. DUBLIN.

ELTIC ORNAMENT.

No period in the history of art is more remarkable than the Celtic. The carved stone architecture and crosses, the bronzes, enamels, and silversmith's work, the splendid illuminated books and manuscripts with capitals and borders full of imagery and intricacy of detail, and the clear and accurate writing of the text are all indications of the culture and love of ornament of the early Irish people, showing a remarkable preference for the spiral and interlacing forms. The bronze shield (fig. 6), with its spirals and bosses of enamel enriched with the northern " Fylfot " is a typical example of the 2nd or 3rd century, A.D. Then comes the trumpet pattern or divergent spiral, which, seen in its infancy on the bronze shield, reached a great degree of elaboration in the 8th and 9th centuries, A.D. (figs. 2 to 7), being typical of Celtic work up to the middle of the 11th century when all trace of this spiral is lost. The interlacing bird and animal forms used from the 8th to the 14th centuries are doubtless derived from Byzantine and Lombardic sources. The serpent or dragon, which is such a marked feature from the 7th to 15th century must have been borrowed from the north, as Ireland had no traditions of snakes or dragons, and it is to Scandinavia, with its legend of Fafni, that we must look for the origin of the dracontine treatment. It is this Zoomorphic character that distinguishes the Celtic from all other styles of ornament except Scandinavian. The obverse of the magnificent processional Cross of Cong (A.D. 1123), is divided into 46 panels of decorations, and convoluted snakes occupy 38 of them.

CELTIC CROSS AT
IRTON, CUMBERLAND.

The illustration given here of the Irton Cross is a typical example of the Celtic ornamentation. The early or Pagan period is noted for its bronze work, cast and wrought, and enriched with Champlevé enamels. The fine chalice of Ardagh (page 133) and the Tara Brooch (plate 60) 7th century, are splendid examples of the Christian period dating from St. Patrick, A.D. 440-460. The beautiful Book of Kells, the Book of Armagh, the Book of Durrow, manuscripts of the early part of the 9th century (Trinity College, Dublin), and the Book of Durham, called the Lindisfarne Gospels, A.D. 689-721, written by Eadfrith, and illuminated by Ethelwald, are a tribute to the vitality, assimilation of ideas, and the culture and wonderful craftsmanship of the early Irish people. In Irish manuscripts gold is not used, except in the Lindisfarne Gospels, where a minute quantity is used.

2
THE OTTERS SKIN
AND THE GOLD.
FROM THE CHURCH
O° GAARDEN GAVELSTAD
LEGEND OF SIGURD
& THE DRAGON.

3 DRACONTINE
ORNAMENT. 1300 A.D

5
BRONZE KNIVES.
COPENHAGEN.
9TH CENTURY.

4 FAFNI THE DRAGON,
AND THE SWORD OF
SIGURD.
A.D 1200

CARVED WOOD PORTALS FROM HYLLESTAD CHURCH.
SETERSDAL A.D 1150 OSLO MUSEUM.

FIG
1.

6
PORTAL OF
DOOR FROM
HEDALS CHURCH
BALDERS. 1400.
CONVOLUTIONS
OF FAFNI.
THE DRAGON
DEVELOPED.

DRACONTINE
ORNAMENT.

7
BROOCH
OF SILVER GILT. 1300 A D
STOCKHOLM MUSEUM.

BRONZE
HATCHET.

8
SILVER BROOCH
DANISH 1400 A D
COPENHAGEN MUSEUM.

SCANDINAVIAN ORNAMENT.

The beautiful bronze and silver jewellery and implements of war of the early Viking period, found in Norway, Sweden, and Denmark, display no trace of plant forms in their ornamentation, the latter consisting wholly of interlacing animal forms—chiefly the dragon. The Viking ship found at Sandifiord in 1880, although destitute of ornament, shows traces of the " Bronze Dragon Prow," referred to in the early Scandinavian Sagas. At the commencement of the 12th century, plant forms are found mingled with the dragons, and figure sculpture became important in treating of the myths of the gods ; Frey, Woden, Thor, and Tyr, of the pagan period, being influenced by the newer cult in religion. This is shown by the Sigurd Overlap, and the story of Sigurd the Volsung.[1]

The farmer Hreithmar had three sons—Otter, Fafni, and Regin the smith ; and three of the Scandinavian gods—Woden, Hœni, and Loki—wandered towards the farm, and, through misunderstanding, Loki killed Otter. For this the three gods were seized, and released only on payment of enough gold to cover the skin of Otter (fig. 2) when hung up by the nose. This price was procured by Loki, who compelled the dwarf Andwari to surrender all the gold he possessed, as well as a magic ring, which carried with it a curse that for eight lives the gold should be fatal to its owner. Then Hreithmar was slain by his surviving sons for the treasure, which was carried off to a great mound on Gnita Heath by Fafni, who lay round his plunder in the form of a dragon. Regin, his brother, in order to obtain the treasure, prompted Sigurd, his foster son, to slay the dragon. Sigurd, in testing his sword, broke it in twain ; thereupon Regin made him a magic sword, with which he lay in the trail of the dragon, and pierced it through (figs. 1-4). Then Regin took out the heart of the dragon, which Sigurd cut into pieces and toasted while Regin slept. Sigurd, burning his fingers, placed them in his mouth, and tasted the blood of Fafni, the dragon (fig. 1), and lo ! he heard the voice of birds saying that Regin was plotting to kill him. Then Sigurd killed Regin, ate the heart of Fafni, placed the treasure on the back of the noble horse Grani, and departed, only to be slain for the gold by Gunnar, who for this crime was cast into the pit of serpents (fig. 1).

This myth explains much of the Scandinavian ornament, for in figs. 1 and 2 the story is told in a series of incidents remarkable for the fertility of invention and dracontine ornamentation. Halton Cross, in Lancashire, and a slab at Kirk Andreas, Isle of Man, illustrate the same subjects, dating from the 11th century. In later times, the dragon becomes more pronounced in character, until in the 14th century it fills the whole portal with the beautiful interlacing ornament (fig. 6).

[1] " The Pagan-Christian Overlap in the North," by H. Colley March, M.D. (Lond.).
" Sigurd the Volsung," by William Morris.

NORMAN & GOTHIC ARCHITECTURE.

English architecture has been broadly divided into periods for the purpose of classifying the styles, the following being the most generally accepted :—

By Sharpe.[1]		A.D.		By Rickman.[2]		A.D.
Roman-	Saxon - -	1066		Norman - - -	1066-1189
esque	Norman - -	1066-1145		Early English - -	1189-1307
	Transitional -	1145-1190		Decorated - - -	1307-1379
Gothic	Lancet - -	1190-1245		Perpendicular - -	1379-1483
	Curvilinear -	1245-1360		Tudor - - -	1483-1546
	Rectilinear -	1360-1550			

Most of our magnificent cathedrals were founded, A.D. 1066-1170, by Norman bishops, some upon the old Saxon foundations, such as Canterbury and York, or near the original Saxon buildings, as at Winchester, or upon new sites, such as Norwich and Peterborough ; and were without exceptions more magnificent erections than those of the anterior period, portions of the older style still existing in many cathedrals, showing the fusion of Roman and Byzantine architecture with the more personal and vigorous art of the Celtic, Saxon, and Scandinavian peoples.

Lincoln is a typical English plan, showing no trace of the semi-circular apsidal arrangement so universal in Norman and French cathedrals. Each vertical division in the nave, the choir, and transept is termed a bay. On plate 16 is an illustration of four typical bays of English cathedrals, showing the development of style from the 12th to the 15th century. The general characteristic of each bay is given separately, but obviously it can only be approximate, as the building of each cathedral was influenced by local considerations, each period necessarily overlapping its predecessor, thus forming a transitional style. For instance, in the choir of Ripon Cathedral the aisle and clearstory have semi-circular Norman windows, and the nave arcading has pointed arches. In the triforium and clearstory arcading, round arches are seen side by side with the pointed arch.

PLAN OF LINCOLN CATHEDRAL

The PIERS—sometimes termed columns—of these bays have

---

[1] " The Seven Periods of Church Architecture," by Edmund Sharpe.
[2] " Gothic Architecture," by Thomas Rickman.

distinctive features which are character-istic of each period of the Gothic develop-ment.

Sketch plans are here given showing the changes that took place in the section of the pier from 1066 to 1500. The same general characteristics are observed in the arch mouldings and string courses.

CHARACTERISTICS OF THE NORMAN PERIOD.

NAVE ARCADING.—The universal use of the round arch, cylindrical or rectangular piers, with semi-circular shafts attached to each face.

RIEVAULX ABBEY.
THE EAST WALL.
LANCET PERIOD.

Capitals cubical and cushion-shaped. Arch mouldings enriched with concentric rows of Chevron and Billet ornament.

TRIFORIUM.—In early work, of one arch. In later work, two or four small arches carried on single shafts under one large semi-circular arch.

CLEARSTORY. — One window, with an open arcading in front, of three arches, the centre one larger and often stilted. This arcade forms a narrow gallery in the thickness of the Clear-story wall. The roof of the nave of wood, flat and panelled, roof of the aisles semi-circular quadripartite vaulting. An ar-cading of semi-circular arches was usually placed upon the wall, under the aisle windows. Early windows are narrow, flush with the external wall, and deeply splayed on the inside. Later windows are re-cessed externally, with jamb-shafts and capitals supporting an enriched moulded arch. A few circular rose windows still remain, of which a fine ex-ample is to be found in Bar-freston Church, Kent.

EARLY ENGLISH OR LANCET PERIOD.

The Lancet or pointed arch universal.

CAPITALS, of three lobed foliage and circular abacus. The pier arch mouldings, alternate rounds and hollows deeply cut and enriched with the characteristic dog's tooth ornament. A hood moulding which terminates in bosses of foliage or sculptured heads invariably surrounds the arch mouldings. This moulded hood when used externally is termed a " Dripstone," and when used horizontally over a square headed window, à " Label."

The TRIFORIUM has a single or double arch, which covers the smaller or subordinate arches, the spandrels being enriched with a sunk or pierced trefoil or quatrefoil. The Triforium piers are solid, having delicate shafts attached to them, carrying arch mouldings of three orders, and enriched with the dog's tooth ornament or trefoil foliage.

The CLEARSTORY lancet windows are in triplets, with an arcading on the inner face of the wall. The vaulting shaft occasionally springs from the floor, but more usually from a corbel above the nave capitals, and finishes under the clearstory string with an enriched capital, from which springs the simple vaulting usually quadripartite or hexapartite in form. Early windows in small churches were arranged in couplets, and at the east end, usually in triplets, with grisaille stained glass.

The example given on the previous page from the east end of Rievaulx Abbey shows a finely proportioned window and its arrangement. Figure sculpture, beautiful and refined in treatment, was frequently used upon external walls.

The figures of Saints and Bishops were placed singly under triangular pediments and cusped arches, of which there are fine examples at Wells, Lichfield, Exeter, and Salisbury (fig. 5, plate 19). Splendid examples of circular rose windows are to be seen in the north and south transepts of Lincoln Cathedral, also at York, but they are comparatively rare in England, while France possesses over 100 of the finest and most important examples of this type. They are to be seen in the Cathedrals of Notre Dame, Paris ; Rouen ; Chartres ; and Rheims.

DECORATED OR GEOMETRIC PERIOD.

In this, the piers have engaged shafts, with capitals having plain mouldings, or enriched with finely carved foliage of the oak, maple, or mallow, seen in perfection at Southwell Minster, which contains the finest carving of this period—1280-1315 (plate 22). The pier arches have mouldings of three orders, also enriched, usually with the characteristic ball flower, or foliage similar to that upon the capitals.

The TRIFORIUM consists of double arches, with subordinate cusped arches adorned with Geometric tracery. The inner arcading of the Clearstory is absent, the one large window being divided by mullions

PETERBOROUGH · LINCOLN · LICHFIELD · WINCHESTER

CLEAR-STORY

TRIFORIUM

AISLE WINDOW

1 · NORMAN   2 · LANCET   3 · GEOMETRIC   4 · PERPENDICULAR

FOUR BAYS OF TYPICAL ENGLISH CATHEDRALS · 12TH TO THE 15TH CENTURY

EARLY GOTHIC SCULPTURE & ARCADING. SALISBURY CATHEDRAL EXTERIOR

5

6 LATE DECORATED WINDOW. BEVERLEY

7 EARLY GOTHIC. WESTMINSTER

8 PERPENDICULAR WINDOW WEST MINSTER

and geometrical tracery, or by equilateral triangles enriched with circular and bar tracery (fig. 3, plate 19). Above the pier capitals an enriched corbel is usually placed from which springs the vaulting shafts, terminating with a richly carved capital under the Clearstory string. The aisle arcading, as a rule, is very beautiful, having geometric tracery and finely proportioned mouldings, the aisle windows with mullions and bold geometric tracery. The circular rose windows of the transepts are typical of this period.

PERPENDICULAR.

The PIERS of this style are lofty and enriched with shallow mouldings carried round the pier arch ; where capitals are introduced they frequently resemble a band round the pier at the springing of the arch, or occasionally they are octagonal in form, and decorated with an angular treatment of the vine. In some instances the upper part of the plain octagonal capital is relieved with an embattlement. The latter is also frequently used as a cresting for the elaborate perpendicular screens, or for relieving the clearstory strings, or on the transoms of the lofty windows.

The TRIFORIUM is absent in this period, the bay consisting of two horizontal divisions only. The CLEARSTORY, owing to the suppression of the Triforium, becomes of more importance. The windows are large and often in pairs, with vertical mullions extending to the arch mouldings of the window head. The aisle windows are similar, and when lofty have horizontal transoms, on which the battlement ornament is displayed. The aisle arcading being also suppressed, all plain wall space was covered with perpendicular surface tracery. Enrichment of this type was used in the greatest profusion upon walls, parapets, buttresses, and arches, also upon the jambs and soffits of doorways. This, together with the use of the four-centred arch, forms the characteristic feature of the Perpendicular.

ITALIAN GOTHIC.

The remarkable growth of the Gothic style during the 13th and 14th centuries was contemporary in England, France, Flanders, Germany, and in a less degree in Italy. One of the most beautiful churches in Italy is S. Maria della Spina, at Pisa, with its rich crocketed spires and canopies, features which were repeated a little later at the tomb of the famous *Scaligers* at Verona. Venetian Gothic is differentiated by the use of the ogee arch with cusps and pierced quatrefoils.

At Venice there are many magnificent examples of Gothic architecture, remarkable for the beautiful central grouping of the windows, arcades, and balconies and the prevalence of the ogee arch, with cusps and pierced quatrefoils and rich foliated capitals. The façade of the Doge's Palace, with its great colonnade of 36 pillars with rich foliated capitals (see Ruskin's " Seven Lamps of Architecture," plate V.), and the Porta della Carta, or entrance, with its magnificent doorway flanked by figures and canopies and surmounted by a traceried window, and gable enriched with exquisitely carved crockets and finials of foliage and figures, are by Bartolommeo Buon (1420-71), who also built the Foscari Palace. Other examples are the Casa, or C'a'd'oro, and the Palazzi Pisani, Conterini Fasan, and Danieli, each with beautiful central grouping of windows, pierced quatrefoil, and rich balconies.

It was in FRANCE and ENGLAND that Gothic architecture reached its culmination. The abbeys and cathedrals, with spires and towers enriched with vigorous and beautiful sculpture, arcadings and canopies, with cusps, crockets, and finials, and the splendid traceried windows, filled with glorious stained glass, are all tributes to the religious zeal and splendid craftsmanship of the middle ages.

The west fronts of the larger cathedrals of France have deeply-recessed triple porches, covered with figure sculpture (page 55, pl. 26), magnificent towers with lofty open tracery, as at Amiens and Rheims, and splendid rose windows, as those at Chartres (an early example of plate tracery), Rheims, Amiens, and the Cathedral and S. Ouen at Rouen, the latter with rich flamboyant tracery.

French cathedrals are invariably of the periapsidal plan, with the semi-circular eastern ambulatory, surrounded by three or five radiating chapels. Aisle chapels also are frequently introduced between the bases of the flying buttresses, giving a greater width across the church. In early cathedrals, the triforium chamber, or upper aisle and its arcade, was similar to English examples ; but early in the 13th century the triforium gallery was reduced to the thickness of the nave wall, and the outer arcading glazed. Later, the triforium-with its glazed arcading, became merged into the great clearstory windows, with their wealth and glory of coloured glass.

English cathedrals show a marked contrast in scale to contemporary French buildings. The English nave and choir are less in height and width but greater in length than French cathedrals. For instance, Westminster is the highest of our English churches, with its nave and choir 103 ft. from floor to roof, 30 ft. wide, and 505 ft. in length. York is next with 101 ft. from floor to roof, 45 ft. wide, and 486 ft. in length. Salisbury is 84 ft. from floor to roof, 32 ft. wide, and 450 ft. in length ; and Canterbury 80 ft. from floor to roof, 39 ft. wide, and 514 ft. in length. Lincoln with 82 ft. and Peterborough with 81 ft. are the only other examples reaching 80 ft. in height : York, with 45 ft., being the only one reaching above 40 ft. in width of nave. The measurements of contemporary French cathedrals, on the other hand, being as follows : Chartres, 106 ft, from floor to roof, 46 ft. wide, and 415 ft. in length ; Notre Dame, 112 ft. from floor to roof, 46 ft. wide, and 410 ft. in length ; Rheims, 123 ft. from floor to roof, 41 ft. wide, and 485 ft. in length ; while Beauvais reaches the great height of 153 ft. being 45 ft. in width, and only 263 ft. in length, the nave never having been built.

1

NORTH
WEST
DOOR·
LINCOLN
CATHEDRAL·

3

BILLET MOULDING

4

ZIGZAG & BALL. LINCOLN.

5

SOUTH
DOOR
KILPECK
CHURCH·
HEREFORD-
SHIRE·

2

BEAK
HEADS
IFFLEY CHURCH

6

ORNAMENT UPON ARCH
St PETERS. NORTHAMPTON

7

CHEVRON
& KEY PATTERN.
DURHAM CATHEDRAL.

8

FRENCH
CAPITAL

9

CAPITAL &
COLUMN AT
WOOTTON.

10

ENRICHMENT FROM THE
JEWS HOUSE LINCOLN

11

FRENCH
CAPITAL

NORMAN ORNAMENT.

Norman Architecture was distinguished by the use of the traditional semi-circular arch, superseded by the pointed arch of the early Gothic period. These semi-circular arches in the earlier dates were decorated with rudely executed carvings, cut or worked with the axe. Later Norman work is very rich, the mouldings being well carved with enrichments of the Chevron, the Cable, Billet, Star, Fret, or Key Patterns ; the Lozenge and the Beading or Pearling. Characteristic features of this period also are the Beakhead (fig. 5), and the Corbel-table, which was a series of heads of men or animals, from which spring small arches supporting the parapet. Many rich examples of Norman surface ornament are still extant ; at Christchurch, Hants, a beautiful intersecting arcading of semi-circular arches occurs, the enrichment above being a scale or imbricated pattern ; at St. Peter's, Northampton, a very rich example of surface ornamentation may be seen (fig. 6).

Floral forms are but rarely used in Norman ornament ; instances are known of the use of the rose and the fir-apple, but they are the exception and not the rule.

Early doorways usually have a square head recessed under semi-circular arch mouldings, decorated with the Chevron, Key, or Beakhead. The semi-circular Tympanum over the door was plain or enriched with rude sculpture in low relief. Later doors show a great profusion of ornament in the archivolt and arch mouldings, which are often carried down the jamb mouldings. The recessed columns are also enriched with the Chevron, or diagonal lines of pearling (fig. 1), and have sculptured capitals showing a classical tendency in the arrangement of acanthus foliage and the volute. Fine examples of this period may be seen in the west front of Lincoln Cathedral (fig. 1), the Galilee porch at Durham, and the west door of Iffley Church, Oxfordshire. A fine, deeply recessed semi-circular Norman doorway is at Tutbury Church, having a richly recessed window over, now filled with flamboyant tracery.

Early Norman capitals are usually cubical or cushion-shaped, with a square or cruciform abacus, or occasionally octagonal as at Durham, or circular as at Gloucester, and enriched with the Chevron, Star, or Anthemion, the Capitals being escalloped with segments of circles, or enriched with Volutes or the Anthemion. Early examples are in the White Tower, and St. Bartholomew, London. Later Capitals, usually rich in ornamentation, are found at St. Peter's, Northampton, and at Wooton, more frequently they have interlacing bands of ornament and animals ; there are others with figures, or " Storied Capitals," as in the North Porch, Wells.

In the transition period—end of 12th century—Capitals were concave or bell-shaped, with foliage of the serrated water-leaf type clinging to the bell and turning up under the abacus, forming a Volute. This foliage was varied in type and vigorous in technique. Fine examples are at Christ Church, Oxford, and at Canterbury Cathedral.

47

2

STONE
BOSS·

1

STONE:
SPANDRIL·
FROM CHANCEL·
ARCADE + STONE
CHURCH · KENT·

3

EARLY GOTHIC GLASS · SALISBURY

4

CROCKET·
YORK·
CATHEDRAL·

5

FROM SALISBURY
CATHEDRAL·

6

FROM
ELY·
CATHEDRAL·

8

TOOTH ORNAMENT·

9

PETERBOROUGH·

DIAPER·
WESTMINSTER·

ELY CATHEDRAL·

10

EARLY
ENGLISH
CLUSTERED
CAPITAL·

LINCOLN
CATHEDRAL·

11

EARLY
FRENCH
GOTHIC·
NOTRE
DAME·

12

EARLY
FRENCH
CAPITAL·
RHEIMS·
CATHEDRAL·

48

EARLY GOTHIC ORNAMENT.

The NORMAN style was succeeded by the pointed, or GOTHIC style, remarkable for its variety, its beauty of proportion, and the singular grace and vigour of its ornament. Showing no traditions, beyond Sicilian and Arabian influence, it grew rapidly, and reached a high degree of perfection in France and England. The massive and barbaric character of the Norman style gave place to the light clustered shafts and well-proportioned mouldings of the early English Gothic, with its capitals characterized by a circular abacus, and the typical three-lobed foliage growing upwards from the necking of the shafts, thence spreading out in beautiful curves and spirals under the abacus. This tendency to the spiral line is peculiar to the early Gothic, and differentiates it from the Decorated and Perpendicular Period. The diagrams of the three crockets here given show the distinctive character of English Gothic ornament.

Early Gothic, three-lobed leaves arranged in spiral lines. Decorated Gothic, with natural types of foliage, such as the oak and maple, with a flowing undulating line. Perpendicular Gothic, showing the vine and leaves as elements, and arranged in a square and angular manner. The same features and characteristics are observed in the borders here given. The carved spandril from the Chancel Arcade, Stone Church, Kent (fig. 1), is one of the most beautiful examples of English ornament, remarkable for the vigour and flexibility of curve, its recurring forms of ornamentation, and admirable spacing, typical of much of our early English foliage from about 1170-1280.

The type of foliage in early English stained glass is somewhat similar to contemporary carved work, but showing more of the profile of the leaf; it has a geometric or radiating arrangement in addition to the spiral forms of foliage (plate 59), and the admirable spacing of the ornament shows the skill in design that the mediæval craftsman possessed.

CAPITALS FROM CHAPTER HOUSE. SOUTHWELL.

FROM THE TRIFORIUM OF NAVE. S? ALBANS.

A MISERERE.

PARAPET, BEVERLEY MINSTER.

THE BALL-FLOWER.

ALTERNATE BALL-FLOWER.

FINIAL & CROCKETS. LINCOLN

CORBEL OF VAULTING SHAFT. EXETER.

FOUR-LEAVED-FLOWER.

DECORATED GOTHIC ORNAMENT.

Decorated Gothic is remarkable for its geometric or curving tracery, its natural types of foliage, and the undulating character of line and form, in its ornamental details. The foliage of the oak, the vine, the maple, the rose, and the ivy were introduced in much luxuriance and profusion, being carved with great delicacy and accuracy. Lacking the dignity and architectonic qualities of the early Gothic foliage, it surpassed it in brilliancy and inventiveness of detail. The capitals, enriched with adaptations from nature, carved with admirable precision, were simply attached round the bell (page 102), giving variety and charm of modelling, but lacking that unity which was so characteristic of early work.

FINIAL & CROCKETS. EXETER CATHEDRAL.

The illustrations from Southwell are characteristic examples of the richly-carved clustered capitals of this period. The arch mouldings were also enriched with foliage of a similar type, and at the springing of the vaulting shaft of the nave, beautiful carved corbels, such as those at Exeter, were used, while the walls, screens, and parapets, were diapered with low relief carving.

Crockets and finials, which were introduced in the early Gothic period, were now treated with exceeding richness and used in the greatest profusion. A characteristic example is given here from Exeter Cathedral.

The three surviving Queen Eleanor crosses (erected 1291-4), at Geddington, Northampton, and Waltham, are perhaps the richest examples of the Decorated period, showing the exuberance of modelling and the versatility and skill of the English craftsman in the finest period of Naturalistic foliage (1280-1315). The statues of Queen Eleanor are by William of Ireland, "imaginator."

The "Ball Flower" so characteristic of the decorated period, replaced the equally characteristic "Tooth Ornament" of the preceding style, and was much used in some buildings, even to excess—as in the south aisle of Gloucester Cathedral. It is found in the hollows round doorways, windows, arches, and canopies, and it has been known to alternate with the "Four-petalled Flower."

WALL DIAPER WEST-MINSTER.

1 CORNICE FROM BISHOP BECKINGTON'S SHRINE WELLS CATHEDRAL

3 TUDOR FLOWER WESTMINSTER

2 FROM UFFORD CHURCH. SUFFOLK

4 FRIEZE FROM ROOD SCREEN TRUNCH CHURCH NORFOLK

5 TRUNCH CHURCH, NORFOLK

6 FROM ROOD-SCREEN SOUTH POOL CHURCH. DEVON

9 SCREEN TO LADY CHAPEL MANCHESTER CATHEDRAL

7 UPPER PART OF SOUTH PORCH. LAVENHAM CHURCH. SUFFOLK

8 FIREPLACE IN TATTERSHALL CASTLE LINCOLNSHIRE 1433-55

SCREEN DETAIL, EDINGTON CHURCH, WILTSHIRE.

SCREEN CARVING, NORTON FITZWARREN, SOMERSET.

PERPENDICULAR GOTHIC.

The latest Gothic style in England is characterized by a verticality of line in construction and ornament. One of several exceptions is the beautiful fan-vaulting, such as that in the cloisters at Gloucester Cathedral, and in Henry VII.'s Chapel at Westminster, which are not approached by any Continental example for beauty of craftsmanship or scientific precision of masonry. The many splendid towers, having elaborate panelled tracery, and capped with pinnacles, open parapets and battlements, such as those at Wrexham and S. Mary's, Taunton, are also characteristic of this period. The windows, with vertical mullions running to the window-head, which is frequently a four-centred arch, have, in large examples, one or more transoms, enriched with battlements or Tudor flowers, to divide the lofty windows horizontally (plate 19). The 15th century carving and detail, especially in woodwork, is gloriously rich and varied, vigorous in design, and of consummate craftsmanship Local schools of marked individuality occur; thus an East Anglian screen is entirely different to one in Devon. The great mass of fine work extant in cathedrals and churches: screens, pulpits, stalls, font-covers, etc., is a great heritage from mediæval times, of which all should be proud, and learn to explore and appreciate. The many choir screens and stalls, with their canopies, have panels, friezes, crestings, and finials, and are frequently carved with treatment of the vine (figs. 1-7), the Tudor flower being prevalent.

The terminals of the ends of stalls were frequently enriched with foliated "Poppy-heads," often of great beauty.

Heraldic forms, such as shields, with their supporters, together with badges and crests, were largely associated with the ornament in the richer buildings of this period, such as King's College Chapel at Cambridge, and Henry VII.'s Chapel at Westminster.

TERMINALS of PEW-ENDS. 'POPPY-HEADS'

Nave piers are usually rectangular or lozenge in section, consisting of a few rounds and double ogee moulds, and an octagonal capital is typically carried by some of the round members of the pier. A common enrichment in the hollows of the strings and arch mouldings is a four-petalled flower, alternate square and circular (figs. 7 and 8).

EARLY GOTHIC STONE CARVING. NOTRE DAME. PARIS.

1

3
13ᵀᴴ CENTURY CAPITAL

4 14ᵀᴴ CENTURY CARVINGS.

5

WOOD CARVING

CANOPY OF
STALLS IN
CATHEDRAL,
AMIENS
LATE GOTHIC.

2

FRENCH GOTHIC ORNAMENT.

French cathedrals show a marked contrast in scale and enrichment to those of England, being wider, shorter, and higher in proportion, and the sculpture bolder, more profuse, and larger in scale than in contemporary English cathedrals. The principal doorways are also on a large scale, and are usually enriched with numerous statues, placed under canopies, which cover the whole of the recessed arch; whilst the central pier of the door, carrying the figure of the Madonna or a bishop, supports the tympanum (the space within the arch), which is also covered with horizontal bands of sculpture. The figure sculpture of the late 13th and early 14th centuries has considerable skill of composition, and well-arranged draperies; broad and simple in mass, and vigorous in execution (page 56).

The gables of the doors are frequently enriched with crockets and finials, or with beautiful open tracery —as in the west doors of Rouen Cathedral. The Cathedral of Amiens has a delightful series of sculptured reliefs of Biblical subjects, called the Bible of Amiens, enclosed within quatre-foil panels, which extends across the lower part of the façade.

The early relief ornament of the 13th century is remarkable for its vigorous carving and boldness of relief. It differs from contemporary English work in having a rounder form of leaf, divided into lobes, with strongly marked radiating mid-ribs (compare fig. 1, plate 25, with fig. 1, plate 21). The capitals, with the foliage clinging closely to the bell (fig. 3) have not the spiral tendency which characterized English ornament of the same period. The abacus is generally square (page 102), and the clustered pillars and the bell-shaped moulded capitals, without foliage, which are typical of English work, are almost unknown in France. In the 14th century, the foliage, like contemporary carving in England, is naturalistic (figs. 4 and 5, plate 25, and page 102), with a ribbed tool-mark following the direction of the leaf.

Among the many splendid examples of the 15th century, or flamboyant period, are the stalls of Amiens (fig. 2), where flowing tracery is intermingled with rich cusped-arches, open gables, and crocketed pinnacles.

55

FRENCH GOTHIC SCULPTURE.

FIGURES FROM WEST FRONT OF
CHARTRES CATHEDRAL,
XII. CENTURY.

PIER FROM WEST DOOR,
AMIENS.

CENTRAL PIER AND PART OF TYMPANUM,
SOUTH DOOR, AMIENS CATHEDRAL,

Plate 26.

A PORTION OF THE ARCHITRAVE, FROM THE BRONZE GATES OF THE BAPTISTERY FLORENCE
BY LORENZO GHIBERTI. 1425-52. QUATTROCENTO PERIOD

2

CORBEL
DUCALE PAL
ACE, URBINO

3

4

DRAWING FOR A FRIEZE BY GIOLAMÓ CURTI 16th Century
IN THE UFFIZI GALLERY FLORENCE BERTEN ORNAMENT

5

PAGE FROM THE BOOK OF HOURS, OF
BONA SFORZA, DUCHESS OF MILAN
1477-90   BRITISH MUSEUM.

6

MARBLE
TABERNACLE
OR SHRINE
BY ANDREA
FERRUCCI
1528.

FROM THE CHURCH OF SAN GIROLAMO AT FIESOLE

7

ORNAMENT FROM THE BERNARDO MONUMENT
IN THE CHURCH OF SANTA MARIA DE' FRARI
VENICE. 1540.

BORDER FROM THE
GRENVILLE SFORZIADA.
1480. BRITISH MUSEUM

8

ENAMELLED TERRA-COTTA OR DELLA ROBBIA WARE
BY LUCA DELLA ROBBIA. 1450
IN THE CHURCH OF S ONOFRIO ROME.

9

PAINTED ORNAMENT FROM THE DUCAL PALACE MANTUA
BY GIOVANNI DA UDINE AND GIULIO ROMANO
1530

ENASCENCE ARCHITECTURE & ORNAMENT IN ITALY.

Lombardy, in the north of Italy, had witnessed a singular blending of the old classic art with the vigorous traditions and myths of the Longobards, and the symbolisms of Byzantium; thus producing the architecture known as Lombardic, with its multiplicity of small columns and arches, quaint imagery of sculpture, and the frequent use of a lion or dragon as a support for the columns. These are features of the early art at Lucca, Bergamo, Padua, Verona, and other towns in Lombardy (see Romanesque, page 35); a beautiful illustration from Lucca is given in the appendix to Ruskin's " Stones of Venice," Vol. I. Contemporary with this period came the Gothic influence, with its clustered columns, pointed arches, its cusps and crockets, and its strong vitality, impressing the arts and architecture with a lasting influence; hence, during the 12th and 13th centuries in Italy, this intermingling of styles, traditions, religious beliefs and myths, produced an art barbaric and vigorous in character, the imagery full of suggestiveness, and the detail rich and varied in conception. Yet it was but the herald of a style which culminated in the epoch of the Renascence, a style where symmetry was to play an important part as in classic art, where refinement of line and detail, of culture and craftsmanship, are found; and which, though beautiful in proportion, unity of parts, and perfect adaptability, yet lacked that symbolism, suggestiveness, inventiveness and rugged strength of the early Byzantine, Lombardic, and Gothic styles.

The earlier Italian Renascence is broadly divided into three periods, viz. : The Tre-Cento, A.D. 1300-1400 ; the Quattro-Cento, 1400-1500 ; and the Cinque-Cento, 1500-1600.

In the Tre-Cento period the sculpture and decorative arts are marked by dignity of conception, and a mingling of Gothic and classic traditions. Two of the earliest examples showing Renascence influence are the hexagonal pulpits in the Baptistery at Pisa and the Cathedral at Siena by Niccolo Pisano. These are transitional in style, having sculptured panels distinctly classical in treatment, associated with cusped Gothic arches. Niccolo also executed the beautiful octagonal fountain at Perugia and was assisted in much of his work by his son Giovanni Pisano, who was the author of the beautiful pulpit in the Cathedral at Pisa. A fine monumental work showing these characteristics is the tomb of S. Peter the martyr in the Church of S. Eustorgio at Milan.

In the architecture, Gothic forms prevail, together with panelling of white and grey marble, lofty pilasters, pinnacles, and gables, enriched with a geometric pattering of marbles or mosaic, and also a frequent use of the twisted pillar.

The Cathedral at Florence (plan, p. 176), with its panelling, pointed arches, and rich tracery, was by Arnolfo di Cambio (died 1300) and

Francesco Talenti, who completed the nave, choir, and apses in 1321. Arnolfo and Talenti were also the architects for the Church of Santa Croce and the Palazzo Vecchio, Florence (1290), where, in 1434, Michelozzo added the beautiful cortile, and C. Salviati and De Faenza, pupils of Vasari, enriched the circular and octagonal pillars with beautiful stucco ornamentation (plate 28), in 1565.

The fine campanile by Giotto (1336), Andrea Pisano, and Francesco Talenti, who introduced the upper Gothic windows, is a noble accessory to the Cathedral of Florence.

In 1293 Arnolfo introduced some Prato marble pilasters at the angles of " San Giovanni," the octagonal Florentine Baptistery, an ancient building where many of the great citizens of the Republic received their baptism; it was here that Dante was baptised in May, 1265.

The last of the Tre-Cento masters was Andrea Pisano, who made the first bronze gate of " San Giovanni," or the Baptistery of Florence. This gate has 28 quatre-foil panels in relief, and bears the inscription " ANDREAS UGOLINI NINI PISIS ME FECIT, A.D. MCCCXXX."

The true Renascence or Quattro-Cento period is remarkable for the vitality of the arts, and the vigour and versatility of its crafts-men. Brunelleschi is the earliest architect (page 68), and Lorenzo Ghiberti the first ornamentist and sculptor, whose chief works are the two bronze gates for the Florentine Baptistery. The first gate (1403-24), has 28 quatre-foil panels similar to the earlier one by

MONUMENT TO ILARIA DEL CARRETTO, BY JACOPO DELLA QUERCIA.

Andrea Pisano, and the last gate (1425-59), has 10 rectangular panels with incidents from the Old Testament in high relief (plate 65).

The styles or framework of these gates, have a series of single figures in niches with circular medallions between them.

The bronze architrave round each of the Ghiberti gates and the
earlier gate by Andrea Pisano, are rich examples of Quattro-Cento
design. The details are natural fruits, flowers and foliage, banded
together with ribbons, with the introduction of birds, squirrels, etc.
The egg-plant and pomegranate portion (fig. 1) is a familiar example.

Other masters of this period were Jacopo della Quercia, who, in
1406, executed the beautiful monument shown on the previous page to
Ilaria di Carretto, in the Cathedral at Lucca. The recumbent figure
of Ilaria is sculptured in white marble with perfect simplicity and
beauty ; another famous work of Jacopo was the fountain at Siena.

Luca della Robbia executed a beautiful organ gallery in marble
for the Cathedral at Florence (1431), now in the museum of the Opera
del Duomo, Florence, with admirable singing and dancing figures, in
relief. Donatello was remarkable for the singular grace and sincerity
of his portraiture, especially of children. The dancing figures in

THE "CANTORIA," OR SINGING GALLERY, BY DONATELLO (1435).

relief on the panels of the singing gallery of the Cathedral of Florence
with which he was commissioned in 1443 are perfect examples of his
art.

This frieze of children is a delightful example of one phase of Donatello's craftsmanship, showing the vitality and exuberance of his
conception. The peculiar relief, called " *stacciato*," of the figures
which shows a series of almost flat surfaces, upon which is carved
exquisitely delicate reliefs, contrasted with an abrupt contour giving
strongly-marked shadows, is typical of much of Donatello's relief-

S. GEORGE, BY DONATELLO.

work. An illustration is also given of the famous S. George, from the Gothic Church or oratory of Or San Michele, Florence. This church has niches and canopies on the external walls, each with its statue by great Quattro-Cento masters. Three statues in marble of S. Peter (1412), S. Mark (1412), and S. George (1415), are by Donatello; three in marble, S. Philip (1408), Four Crowned Martyrs, and S. Eligius (1415), by Nanni di Banco; S. John (1415), S. Matthew (1422), and S. Stephen (1428), in bronze, by Ghiberti; Christ and S. Thomas (1483), bronze, by Verrochio; and S. Luke (1601), in bronze, by Giovanni da Bologna.

The Monastery of San Marco is one of the remarkable buildings in Florence. Built in 1437-50 by Michelozzo for Cosimo de Medici, it was enriched with the most beautiful frescoes by Fra Angelico.

The art of the medallist, which had declined since the time of the Roman Empire, now took its position among the arts of the Quattro-Centro period, under Vittore Pisano, called Pisanello. The vigour of his modelling and the individuality of his medals of the contemporary princes of Italy, are exceedingly fine. Among other remarkable medallists, were Sperandio of Verona, Caradossa of Milan. Vincentine of Vicenza, Benvenuto Cellini of Florence, Lione Leoni, Pompeoni Leoni, and Pastorino of Siena.

Other names of this period were Desiderio da Settignano, his master-

RELIEFS FROM THE SINGING GALLERY, BY DONATELLO, IN THE MUSEUM OF THE OPERA DEL DUOMO, FLORENCE.

piece being the tomb of Carlo Marsuppini, in the Church of Santa Croce, Florence ; Mino da Fiesole ; Andrea Verrocchio, the author of the fine equestrian statue of Bartolomeo Colleone at Venice (see Bronzes, plate 65) ; Matteo Civitali ; and the Rossellini, a remarkable family of five brothers, of which the most famous was Antonio Rossellino, who executed a charming tomb to Cardinal Jacopo di Portogallo, in the Church of the Nunziata, Florence.

The Cinque-Cento period was the culmination of the Renascence, when architecture, sculpture, painting, and the decorative arts, were under the munificent patronage of the popes and princes of Italy. Palaces, churches, and public buildings were completed (see Renascence Architecture, pages 68-70), and embellished with beautiful sculptures and decorations ; hung with the most sumptuous fabrics of the Venetian, Florentine, and Genoese looms ; decorated with altar paintings and mural decorations by the most renowned of painters ; and enriched with the magnificent productions of the gold and silversmiths' art, and the lovliest of intarsia, or inlaid woodwork.

THE CUMÆAN SIBYL
BY MICHEL ANGELO

The Sistine Chapel, built for Sixtus IV., in 1473, by Baccio Pintelli, is decorated with fresco paintings on the walls by the great Cinque-Cento masters, Luca Signorelli, Sandro Botticelli, Cosimo Rosselli, Perugino, the master of Raphael, Domenico Ghirlandajo, and Michel Angelo, who painted " The Last Judgment " on the end wall, and the famous ceiling, with incidents from the Old Testament, and with the prophets Joel, Ezekiel, Jeremiah, Jonah, Daniel, Isaiah, and Zechariah, and the sibyls Erithræa, Perscia, Lybica, Cumæa, and Delphica. These are splendid examples of decorative painting, where unity and dignity of conception, powerful draughtsmanship, and marvellous execution are shown in a remarkable degree.

The New Sacristy of San Lorenzo, Florence, designed and executed by Michel Angelo, having the tombs of Lorenzo and Giuliano de Medici, with the reclining figures of Dawn and Twilight, Day and Night, shows his remarkable versatility, power, and conception of art.

The art of mural decoration reached its highest degree of achievement during this period in the hands of Raffaele and his contemporaries. The earliest Fresco paintings by the Quattro-Cento masters, such as those in the Arena Chapel at Padua and the Church of San

MARBLE FRIEZE.   CHURCH OF SANTA MARIA DEI MIRACOLI, VENICE. by P. LOMBARDO.

PORTION OF
OCTAGONAL COLUMN
with STUCCO ENRICHMENT.
PALAZZO VECCHIO.
FLORENCE.

MARBLE PANEL. S. MICHELE, VENICE. by P. LOMBARDO.

PART OF TERRA
COTTA PILASTER.

SANTA MARIA DEI MIRACOLI.

TOMB OF LORENZO DE MEDICI,
SACRISTY OF SAN LORENZO, FLORENCE.

Francesco at Assisi by Giotto, and the series of panels by Benozzo Gozzoli in the Chapel of the Riccardi Palace at Florence undoubtedly exercised a stimulating influence upon the Cinque-Cento masters, but a more potent influence was the discovery of the ancient baths of Titus, and the house of Livia with their arabesques and mural paintings.

These antique painted arabesques, or, as they were termed, *Grotteschi*, were now utilized and developed to an extraordinary degree of richness and diversity of type. Pinturicchio was probably one of the first masters to use this arabesque type in the decoration of the Papal apartments in the Castle of Sant Angelo at Rome (1494) for Pope Alexander VI. Pinturicchio, doubtless with other artists in collaboration, also carried out the decoration of the Cathedral Library at Siena, one of the most complete decorative schemes in Italy.

It was, however, at the Vatican that decorative art, especially arabesque painting, reached its highest development under Raffaele and his school, in the decoration of the Loggia of the Court of S. Damaso (1515-20). This open Loggia of three storeys (plate 29) was decorated under the supervision of Raffaele, with whom many artists collaborated, chief among them being Giovanni da Udine, Giulio Romano, Francesco Penni, and Perino del Vaga.

The first and second storeys of this Loggia are roofed with low cupolas. In the first storey the cupolas are decorated by Giovanni da Udine, two with trellis work alternate with one with coffered panels. The second storey is the most richly decorated (plate 29), the walls, piers, pilasters, and ceilings being covered with arabesques. In the cupolas of the ceiling are small rectangular panels painted by Raffaele with Scriptural subjects, and called Raffaele's Bible. The arabesques are painted in polychrome, chiefly in the secondary colours, on a light ground, with panels painted with festoons of fruit on a dark blue ground by Giovanni da Udine.

The third storey was also largely the work of da Udine (1520-30), but in 1580 Padre I. Danti painted upon the walls maps of ancient and modern Italy, and Tempesta and Paul Briel, towns and landscapes.

Modelled stucco work took a most important part in framing the pilasters and panels of this loggia, doubtless under the direction of Giovanni da Udine, for Giorgio Vasari writes:—" One Pietro Lorenzo Luzzi, a youth from Feltri, studied many of the graves and grottos, and earned for himself the name of Morto di Feltri. He re-introduced into ornamental art Stucco and Sgraffito, for although it may have been by Giovanni da Udine and other artists who are now distinguishing themselves, that these decorations have been brought to their ultimate perfection, yet it is not to be forgotten that our first thanks and commendations are due to Morto di Feltri, who was the first to discover and restore the kind of painting we call ' grotesque,' seeing that they were for the most part hidden among the subterranean portions of the ruins of Rome whence he brought them."

Morto went to Florence and with Andrea di Cosimo executed at the Gondi Palace the first *sgraffito* decorations.

Contemporaneously with the Loggie of the Vatican, the Stanze, a series of four rooms, was enriched with mural paintings by Raffaele. His first mural painting here was the " Disputa " (1508) in the Camera della Segnatura, followed by the " Poetry, Philosophy, or School of Athens " and " Jurisprudence," the ceiling being painted with figures and arabesques by Sodoma (Bazzi). The Stanze of Heliodorus (1514) has the " Expulsion of Heliodorus from the Temple," " Miracle of Bolsena," " Leo I. and Attila," and the " Deliverance of S. Peter." In the Stanze Incendio del Borgo (1517), are the " Incendio del Borgo Vecchio," the " Justification of Leo III., before Charlemagne," the " Coronation of Charlemagne by Leo III.," and the " Victory of Leo IV. over the Saracens." Perino del Vaga and Giovanni da Udine assisted Raffaele in the last two paintings. The mural paintings for the Sala of Constantine were designed by Raffaele, but were carried out by his pupils, Giulio Romano, Francesco Penni, and Raffaele del Colle.

With the death of Raffaele in 1520 and the completion of the decorations, the Vatican School with its splendid tradition of artistic resource and skill was largely requisitioned by the nobles of Rome and North Italy for the embellishment of their palaces, the most important example of civic patronage being the decoration of the Farnesina Palace (1510-24) by Baldassare Peruzzi, Giulio Romano, Giovanni

ARABESQUES FROM THE SECOND FLOOR.

ELEVATION TO COURT.

LOGGIA OF THE VATICAN.

SECTION THROUGH LOGGIA.

da Udine, and G. Razzi.   The upper storey of the palace was decorated by Romano and Da Udine with the story of Psyche designed by Raffaele.   Da Udine also carried out the magnificent decorations of the Villa Madama (1520-4), where there is some of the finest stucco enrichments of this period.   The best example of decorative painting by Peruzzi is the Villa Belearo, Siena (1535).

Giulio Romano entered the service of Federigo Gonzaga, Duke of Mantua.   He enriched with paintings and arabesques the Palazzo Ducale and the Palazzo del Tè.   Perino del Vaga carried the art to Genoa, decorating with arabesques and medallions the Palazzo Andrea Doria.

Francesco Primaticcio, who for six years was Giulio Romano's chief assistant at Mantua, was in 1531 invited by Francis I. to Fontainebleau, where he decorated the Great Gallery, or the Gallery of Ulysses, with the subjects from the " Odyssey," together with many delicate reliefs.

All these Italian painted arabesques show a great inventiveness and skilful combination of parts, but they are not to be compared with the refined and beautiful modelling, and harmonious composition of the contemporary carved reliefs by Andrea Sansovino, Jacopo Sansovino, Agostino Busti, Pietro Lombardo, and his sons Tullio and Antonio.   These delicate reliefs have the traditional Roman acanthus, but treated with a refined feeling for modelling, and beauty and symmetry of line and mass.

THE TRIUMPH OF JULIUS CÆSAR FRIEZE BY ANDREA MANTEGNA

In many examples, vases, masks, shields, and similar accessories are found in profusion (plate 28).   The composition of the Cinque-Cento ornament is usually symmetrical, the details being varied and interesting in the best examples.

Andrea Mantegna (circ. 1430—d. 1506), who possessed a romantic passion for the antique, executed nine paintings or cartoons in tempera upon linen, representing the triumphs of Julius Cæsar, which are a portion of a frieze 9 ft. high and 80 ft. long, painted for Lodovico Gonzaga's Palace of S. Sebastian at Mantua. They were purchased by Charles I. and are now at Hampton Court. An illustration of this frieze, from an engraving upon copper in the British Museum, is given here.   It was also engraved on wood by Andrea Andreani in 1599.

The study of classical architecture was stimulated by the publication at Rome, in 1486, of the treatise by Vitruvius, an architect of the time of Augustus ; an edition was also published at Florence in 1496, and at Venice in 1511.   In 1570, Fra Giocondo, at Venice, published " The Five Books of Architecture," by Andrea Palladio.

Another treatise upon architecture, by Serlio, was also published at Venice in 1537 and 1540.

Beautiful types of the Renascence decorative art were the Venetian well-heads, situated in most of the public squares of Venice, and in many of the court-yards of her princely palaces. Designed with details of the most varied and beautiful character by such artists as Andrea Sansovino, Pietro Lombardo, and his sons Tullio and Antonio, the Venetian well-head became a type of beauty, diversified in its treatment, but never losing its characteristics or its usefulness.

The earlier examples are square or circular, with enrichments of Byzantine character, consisting largely of interlacing, circular, and angular lines, enclosing quaint bird and animal forms. In the later examples the Renascence treatment is used with singular richness and appropriateness, the grace, delicacy and diversity of detail

MARBLE WELL-HEAD FROM S S BARNABA — IN THE MUSEUM VENICE

being a tribute to the vivacity and artistic feeling of the Venetian Republic. These well-heads, worked mostly in white marble and evincing good judgment in the quality of relief, now show comparatively little injury after centuries of usefulness. Occasionally they were of bronze, like the two fine examples still in position in the courtyard of the Doge's Palace.

Many of these well-heads are carefully treasured in our European Museums, teaching us that beauty of form, and perfection and delicacy of ornament are quite compatible with usefulness, when used by an artistic people.

RENASCENCE ARCHITECTURE IN ITALY.

The Renascence in Italy was distinguished by the many magnificent ecclesiastical and secular buildings erected during the 15th and 16th centuries in the chief cities in Italy. Florence was the first to show activity, and with Brunelleschi the history of Renascence architecture commences. The great dome of the Cathedral (1420-34), the Pazzi Chapel (with a fine frieze of cherubs' heads by Donatello and Settignano) at S. Croce (1420), and the Church of S. Lorenzo (1425), were his first works, and were followed by S. Spirito (1433) and the Pitti Palace.

The severe dignity of the bold rusticated stone work, which was usually varied in each storey, the circular-headed windows, and cornices of great depth and projection, became the type of the early palaces of Florence and Siena.

The first Renascence palace was the Riccardi, built for Cosimo de Medici, in 1430, by Michelozzi; and it was followed by the Pitti

(1435) and the Quaratesi (1442), by Brunelleschi; the Rucellai (1451), by Leon Battista Alberti, where pilasters with their entablature were used for the first time in a Renascence façade; the Strozzi (1489), by B. da Majano and Cronaca; the Gondi (1490), by G. da San Gallo; the Guadagni (1490), with *sgraffito* decorations in grey and white plaster; and the Nicolini, by Bramante, the Pandolfini (1520), by Raphael; and the Bartolini (1520), by Baccio d'Agnolo. The plan of these palaces was usually a rectangle, having an internal cortile, with open arcades on the ground floor, the next floor having windows, while the upper storey was sometimes open.

In Rome the palaces were characterized by largeness of scale, the frequent use of the pilaster or attached super-imposed columns, and square-headed windows, with triangular or segmental pediments The plan is rectangular, with a cortile of one or more storeys of open arcades of semi-circular arches, springing direct from the capital, as in the Cancelleria Palace.

The chief palaces are the Cancelleria (1495) and the Giraud (1503), by Bramante, the Farnesina (1511), the Massimi (1529), and the Villa Ossoli (1525), by Baldassare Peruzzi; the Farnese (1517), by Antonio da San Gallo; the Villa Madama (1516), by Raffaelle and Giulio Romano; the Borghese (1590), by Martino Lunghi; the Laterano (1586), by Fontana; and the Barberini (1626), by Maderna, Borromini, and Bernini.

The chief ecclesiastical building is S. Peter's (plan, plate 85), commenced in 1450 by Alberti and Rossellino for Pope Nicholas V.; then carried on by Bramante and San Gallo (1503), Raphael and Peruzzi (1514-20), Antonio da San Gallo (1534), Michel Angelo (1546), Vignola (1556), Giacomo della Porta (1590), and Carlo Maderna (1608). In 1627 S. Peter's was dedicated by Urban VIII., and in 1667 the colonnade in the piazza was erected by Bernini.

The architecture of Venice is rich and varied in style, and the great *palazzi* of the Byzantine, Gothic, and Renascence periods bear tribute to the versatility and skill of the Venetian architects and craftsmen.

The Renascence period may be said to commence with Pietro Lombardo, who built Santa Maria dei Miracoli (1480), a building remarkable for the singular grace and refinement of the internal carved enrichments (plate 28). Another work by Lombardo was the Spinelli Palace (1480), which has mullioned windows, grouped centrally as in the Gothic palace. This feature, together with the use of pilasters or attached columns, became the type of the later Renascence palaces, such as the Palazzo Vendramini, also by Pietro Lombardo. Then followed the rebuilding of the courtyard of the Ducal Palace by Antonio-Bregni (1485), which was completed in 1550 by Scarpagnino; the Scuola di San Marco (1485) by Martino Lombardo; the Palazzo Cornaro (1532), La Zecca (1536), the Loggetta of the Campanile (1540), destroyed by the falling of the Campanile in 1905, but rebuilt, and the Library of S. Mark (1536), by Jacopo

THE PALAZZO VENDRAMINI, VENICE, BY PIETRO LOMBARDO.

Sansovino; the Grimani Palace (1549) by San Michele; the Pesaro Palace (1650) and the Church of Santa Maria della Salute (1631) by Baldassare Longhena.

Andrea Palladio of Vicenza was the most famous of the later architects of the Renascence. His chief works are the Basilica Vicenza (1549), which has a fine elevation of two super-imposed orders of attached columns, with arched open-

ings and coupled columns in each storey; the Valmarana (1556), the Chiericati (1560), and the Tiene (1565) palaces; and the Teatro Olimpico (1580); all of which are in Vicenza.

In his later work, which is frequently built of brick and stucco, he adopted the device occasionally used by Peruzzi and San Michele, of an attached column, with or without pede-stal, reaching throughout the two storeys of the full height of the building, as in the Casa del Diavolo, Vicenza.

Scamozzi, of Vicenza, succeeded Palladio. He built the Trissino at Vicenza (1588), the Procuratie Nuove (1584), at Venice, and com-pleted Palladio's Church of San Giorgio Maggiore at Venice.

CASA DEL DIAVOLO
VICENZA (PALLADIO).

70

PALAZZO VERZI, VERONA.

ENTRANCE HALL TO THE PALACE OF THE UNIVERSITY AT GENOA.

71

EARLY RENASCENCE SCREEN. CLUNY MUSEUM.

FRONT OF COFFER. PERIOD OF LOUIS XII. CLUNY MUSEUM.

CARVED WOOD PANEL
CLUNY MUSEUM.

PANEL OF DOOR ST MACLOU,
ROUEN. BY JEAN GOUJON

PANELS FROM LIMOGES CATHEDRAL.

FRENCH RENASCENCE.

At the close of the 15th century the Italian Renascence began to exert its influence upon the vigorous and beautiful Gothic art of France, Charles VIII. (1483-89) inviting the Italians, Fra Gioconda, Paganino, Boccador, and various Italian craftsmen to assist in building the castle at Amboise.

At first the influence of the Italian Amboise School was confined to the smaller architectural features, but at the commencement of the 16th century, the classic orders of architecture and the delicate arabesques of Italy, were incorporated with the high-pitched roofs, mullioned windows, dormers, crocketed gables and pinnacles of the beautiful flamboyant Gothic, and fused into the style known as the French Renascence, which is usually divided into distinct characteristic periods, viz. :—I., François Premier, 1515-47 ; II., Henri Deux and Henri Quatre, 1547-1610 ; III., Louis Treize, 1610-43 ; IV., Louis Quatorze, 1643-1715 ; V., Louis Quinze, (1710-70) ; VII., Louis Seize, 1774-89 ; and VIII., The Empire, 1790-1830.

ANCIEN HÔTEL
D'ECOVILLE
CAEN.

Typical examples of the early Renascence architecture are seen in the numerous châteaux planned upon the earlier type of fortified house, that of Chambord (1526), which is singularly flamboyant in style, has circular towers at the angles and flanking the entrance, with a roof of cones and cupolas having high dormer windows and chimneys.

The Italian influence received a stimulus from François I., who in 1530 invited Il Rosso to the palace of Fontainebleau, and Rosso was followed, in 1531, by the painter, Francesco Primaticcio. The decoration of " Galerie de François Ier " in this palace by these Italians consists of figure subjects in fresco, surrounded with cartouches, and figures in stucco. A panel (fig. 1, plate 32) is a representative example of this period, showing the emblem of the King, a salamander, in a cartouche. Emblems of the various kings and queens are important decorative features in French Ornamental Art.

73

PANEL HOTEL DE VILLE, BORDEAUX. LOUIS XVI.

PAINTED PANEL BY JEAN BÉRAIN GALERIE D'APOLLON, LOUVRE LOUIS XIV.

SILK BORDER. THE EMPIRE PERIOD. 1805.

CARVED PANEL BY F. STIEBECQ. GALERIE DE FRANÇOIS Ier FONTAINEBLEAU

FRANCORVM REX

FRANCIS CVS

FRENCH RENASCENCE. Plate 32.

DESIGN FOR A PAINTED CEILING, WITH THE MONOGRAM OF WILLIAM III.
BY DANIEL MAROT, *ca.* 1700.

DETAIL OF ROCOCO WOOD-CARVING ROUND A MIRROR IN THE MINISTRY OF PUBLIC WORKS, PARIS.

FRENCH SILK TEXTILES, LOUIS XVI PERIOD,
USED AS WALL COVERINGS.

Plate 35.

In 1541 the architect Sebastiano Serlio, and the goldsmith Benvenuto Cellini, joined the " School of Fontainebleau," which undoubtedly exercised a controlling influence upon the contemporary French architects, Jacques Androuet du Cerceau, Pierre Lescot, Philibert de l'Orme, and Jean Bullant, and the sculptor Jean Goujon.

The Louvre was commenced by Lescot, who built the south-west angle, which was enriched with sculpture by Goujon. These two also collaborated in the building of the beautiful Fontaine des Innocents at Paris (1550), with its fine low relief panels of draped figures.

The reign of Henri II. was a period of remarkable activity in the Arts ; during this reign and that of Henri IV., the prevalence of interlaced strap-work, delicate reliefs, and the liberal use of the cartouche are the characteristic features. These are seen in the Oiron or Henry Deux pottery (plate 56), the geometrical interlacings of the Grolier bindings (plate 73), and the book illustrations of Orance Fine and Jean Cousin.

The Ballroom or " Galerie de Henri II." at Fontainebleau has a richly coffered ceiling of wood by de l'Orme, and the wall painted in fresco by Primaticcio (1564). P. de l'Orme commenced the Tuileries, and Du Cerceau and Duperiac continued the building of the Louvre.

During the Louis Treize period, the tradition of fine architecture and ornament continued, but was considerably influenced by the Spanish and Flemish barocco. The Luxembourg Palace was built by Salomon de Brosse in 1615-24. Other architects of this period were Jacques le Mercier, who continued the Louvre, and François Mansart, who built the new wing at Blois.

The decorative work was chiefly under the control of Simon Vouet, a prolific painter and designer who largely used the " barocco " style characterised by a twisted and broken cartouche, together with masks and a massive type of arabesque. The beautiful book-bindings by the brothers Eve (plate 73) are fine examples of the more delicate ornamentation of this period.

Louis le Vau, the architect, and Charles le Brun, the painter, were the chief men who controlled the arts during the early period of the long reign of Louis Quatorze, Jules Hardouin Mansard, Jean le Pautre, and Jean Berain during the later period. Le Vau continued the building of the Louvre, the Tuileries, and Versailles, and Le Brun painted his finest decorative work in the " Galerie d'Apollon " at the Louvre, and the " Galerie des Glaces " at Versailles (1662-84), which was re-modelled by Mansart in 1680.

The voluminous festoons and arabesques of Le Pautre and Jean Berain (plates 32 and 74), the beautiful Rouen pottery by Louis Poterat, and the inlaid furniture by André Boulle, are representative of the decorative arts during the latter part of the reign of Louis Quatorze, one of the most important architectural works being the colonnade and east front of the Louvre by Claude Perrault.

1

2

ROCOCO OR LOUIS QUINZE.
WOOD CARVING. NOTRE DAME.

PANEL IN CARVED WOOD.

3

4

TROPHIES OF ARMS BY GIRARDON.   VERSAILLES.

(I) DETAIL OF STUCCO ORNAMENTAL PANEL, FROM THE HÔTEL
DE LA BOURSE AT NANTES.

(2) DETAIL OF PLASTER FRIEZE, FROM THE CHAMBRE DES NOTAIRES
AT NANTES.

(3) BED, FROM THE HÔTEL BEAUHARNAIS, PARIS.

The REGENCY, under the Duke of Orleans, was a period remarkable for the development of the " Rocaille," or Rococo, type of ornament in the hands of Just Aurèle Meissonier and Gilles Marie Oppenord. In this *rocaille*, or scroll and shell work, symmetry was systematically avoided, the ornament showing no restraint or reticence of line or detail, reliance being placed upon the brilliancy and playfulness of modelling and design for effect.

The " rocaille " of the Regency continued to be the chief decorative feature of the LOUIS QUINZE. Rooms had shallow vertical panelling, the lines formed of broken curves and scrolls terminating in shell forms and ribbons (plate 34). The acanthus is replaced by the palm as the chief element in the ornamentation, which in spite of its shallow pretence, is attractive, and was in keeping with the social and civic life of the period. J. Verberckt, Nicolas Pineau, and Jules-Antoine Rousseau are the chief carvers associated with the decorative work of the Louis Quinze.

The architecture, unlike the ornamentation, had a greater severity and dignity of style in the hands of Robert de Cotte, Germain Boffrand, and Ange Jacques Gabriel, the latter being the architect of the Place Louis XV. and of the Petit Trianon (1762-68), one of the most perfect small houses of this period.

Under LOUIS SEIZE, insistence is laid upon symmetry in the arrangement of the ornament, and reticence and delicacy of treatment in the details, which consist of the olive, myrtle, and the lily, with swags and garlands and flowers interwoven with ribbons. The cartouche is eliminated, and the oval medallion or tablet takes its place. Room decorations were frequently in pale colours or white and gold, with delicate stucco or painted ornament and panels. Distinguished ornamentists of this period were Delafosse, Cauvet, Salembier, Lalonde, with the *ebenistes* Riesener and David Roentgen and Gouthière, the worker in metal. Representative architects are Jules Nicolas Servandony, and Soufflot, the architect of S. Geneviève (Panthéon).

The period known as the EMPIRE was one of artistic activity characterized by a cold classic formalism founded upon Greek and Roman models. The elements of the ornamentation were the anthemion, acanthus (plate 37), pateræ, urns, and cornucopias, intermingled with the palm and olive symmetrically arranged, frequently arranged upon diagonal lines, with circular medallions and lozenge shapes.

The chief artists of this period were Charles Normand the architect, and Charles Percier, who in collaboration with P. L. Fontaine, controlled the principal decorative work.

AN ANTHEMION FRIEZE BY P. N. BEAUVALLET, 1820.

DESIGN FOR
A TIME-METRE
BY HOLBEIN. 1544

CANOPY TO STALLS
S.T CROSS. WINCHESTER
1528

WOODCARVING. ASTON HALL

PORTION OF
CEILING AT
ASTON HALL.
BIRMINGHAM

PORTION OF HENRY VII TOMB
BY TORRIGIANO
WESTMINSTER
ABBEY

PANEL FROM THE CHICHESTER TOMB. PILTON CHURCH. DEVON
1566

STONE CARVING. CREWE HALL. CHESHIRE.

(1) PLASTER CEILING FROM THE STAR HOTEL, GREAT YARMOUTH.

(2) PLASTER CEILING FROM THE REINDEER HOTEL, BANBURY, OXON.
[*Both now removed to America.*]

ENGLISH RENASCENCE.

The Renascence commenced in England in the early part of the 16th century, about a hundred years later than that in Florence. The first important work was the tomb of John Young, in terra cotta, originally in the Rolls' Chapel, now in the Record Office Museum, Chancery Lane, completed in 1516 by Pietro Torrigiano, who also executed the fine tomb of Henry VII. (1512-18) in Westminster Abbey. This consists of a rectangular sarcophagus of black marble, on which rest the bronze effigies of the king and his consort. On the sarcophagus are gilded bronze pilasters and circular panels in relief, surrounded with wreaths of black marble (plate 38). The tomb of Margaret, Countess of Richmond, and the high altar and baldachino of black and white marble in the Abbey are also by Torrigiano.

Contemporary with Torrigiano was Benedetto da Rovezzano, of Florence, who was commissioned by Cardinal Wolsey, in 1520, to make a sarcophagus of black touchstone, with a recumbent figure of Wolsey in bronze. On the Cardinal's fall, Henry VIII. commissioned Rovezzano to alter and elaborate the work ; but it was left incomplete, and in 1646 the bronze was sold, and this sarcophagus became the resting-place of Nelson in 1806, and is now in S. Paul's Cathedral. Another Florentine, Giovanni di Majano, modelled some terra-cotta medallions for Wolsey at Hampton Court (1521).

In the work of Hans Holbein (plate 38) the Italian feeling is still retained, showing but little of the Gothic tradition ; but in the middle of the century there came a marked change in the ornamental details, the cartouche and strap work, features common to the developed French, Flemish, and German Renascence becoming a pronounced feature of the English Renascence (plate 38).

A typical early Tudor house consisted of a series of rooms placed irregularly round an open court having an entrance gateway flanked by octagonal towers ; the principal room was the lofty hall with its screen and traceried windows. Oxburgh Hall, Norfolk (1482) and Hengrave Hall, Suffolk (1538), are representative of these Tudor houses.

The famous Elizabethan and Jacobean manor-houses are characterized by regularity and symmetry in plan and elevation. The chief buildings of the Elizabethan period are Charlecote (1558), Longleat (1567), Kirby Hall (1570-75), Montacute House (1580), Wollaton Hall (1580-88), and Hardwick Hall (1597). Of the Jacobean period there are Holland House (1607), Hatfield (1611), Audley End (1615), Aston Hall (1620), and Blickling Hall (1620), with their long galleries and rectangular mullioned windows—characteristic features of the Elizabethan and Jacobean period. There are magnificent circular bay windows at Kirby Hall, Burton Agnes (1602-10), and Lilford Hall (1635), and fine octagonal bays at Astley Hall.

CARVED PANEL FROM THE CHURCH OF ST MARY, BUILT BY WREN, 1695. SOUTH KENSINGTON MUSEUM.

FRIEZE FROM THE CHOIR STALLS, ST PAUL'S.

PANEL IN STONE. NORTH PORCH. ST PAUL'S CATHEDRAL.

DOOR-HEAD CLIFFORDS INN

DOOR-HEAD FROM CLIFFORDS INN.

CARVED FIRE-PLACE IN OAK & CEDAR, FROM A ROOM AT CLIFFORDS INN, LONDON. 1686. NOW IN THE SOUTH KENSINGTON MUSEUM.

FRIEZE OF THE UPPER ORDER OF THE BANQUETING HOUSE, WHITEHALL, BY INIGO JONES. 1622.

The top panel is from ST. MARY, SOMERSET, Upper Thames Street, London, now pulled down except the Tower.

(1) FROM THE WHITE ROOM, WESTWOOD PARK, WORCESTERSHIRE.

(2) FROM HOLYROOD PALACE, EDINBURGH.

(3) FROM THE CHAPEL GALLERY, BELTON HOUSE, LINCOLNSHIRE.

John Thorpe, whose drawings are dated 1570-1621, and Robert Smithson with drawings 1599-1631, are the chief names associated with architectural documents of this period.

Some beautiful ceilings, consisting of geometrical panelling fan-tracery, and pendentives, were similar to wood and stone ceilings of the late Gothic period. These richly-moulded pendentives were connected together with moulded ribs. The ribs frequently had a repeating pattern impressed while the plaster was soft (plate 39). Occasionally a double frieze was used, the lower having delicate arabesques and strap-work, while the upper one had boldly-marked cartouches and arabesques. One of the most important examples of early Renascence plaster is the frieze in the presence chamber, Hardwick Hall. It is decorated with hunting subjects, as Diana and her train, surrounded with forest foliage. This freize is 11 ft. in height, modelled in low relief, and coloured in tempera.

Inigo Jones introduced the purely Italian Renascence. He was known from 1604-30 as the designer for the elaborate scenery for the brilliant masques by Ben Johnson that were performed by the nobles and court of that period. In 1622 Inigo Jones completed the Banqueting House, Whitehall, the only portion of his great design which was carried out. He also designed the Water Gate, York House, executed by his favourite carver, Nicholas Stone ; the Queen's House, Greenwich ; and the great room at Wilton, with its fine mantelpiece and panelling.

The ornament of Inigo Jones is excellent in proportion, and Italian in type. The decoration of the panels and friezes consisted of boldly designed festoons, masks, and shields. The plaster ceilings have large rectangular, circular, or oval panels, with massive moulded ribs enriched with classical detail or with fruit or flowers in relief.

In the work of Wren, which followed, the details are less refined in type, being largely under the influence of realistic ornament and the Dutch School (plate 41).

The era of church building began with Sir Christopher Wren in 1666, after the great fire of London, in which old S. Paul's, ninety-three parish churches and chapels, the Exchange, the Guildhall, and fifty of the City Companies' halls were destroyed. S. Mary le Bow (1680), S. Bride's (1680), S. Clement Dane (1684), and S. Stephen's, Walbrook, illustrate some of the typical features of the fifty-one parochial churches that he designed, and his masterpiece, S. Paul's (1675-1710), is a noble example of English Renascence (plan, page 85). Wren also built portions of Hampton Court and Greenwich Hospital. Nicholas Hawksmoor, a pupil of Wren, built S. George's-in-the-East (1723), Spitalfields Church (1729), and S. George's, Bloomsbury (1730). Castle Howard (1714) and Blenheim Palace are by Sir John Vanbrugh ; S. Philip, Birmingham (1710), by Archer ; Burlington House (1717) by Campbell, who also brought out his great work on English architecture, " Vitruvius Britannicus " (Vol. I., 1715, Vol. II., 1717, Vol.

LIBRARY
CEILING
BY THE
BROTHERS
ADAM.

SPANDRIL OF
BRONZE STOVE-GRATE
BY ALFRED STEVENS.

DOOR PANEL BY
ROBERT ADAM.

BORDERS BY GODFREY SYKES.

DESIGN FOR A POMPEIAN CEILING (V. & A.M.).

ADAM'S DESIGN FOR A CEILING AT CULZEAN CASTLE, SCOTLAND.

A LONDON CEILING OF ADAM TYPE.

III., 1725, whole Vols. IV. and V. were issued by Woolfe and Gandon in 1767). This book gives introductory descriptions, with plans, elevations, and sections of the chief English buildings erected between 1600-1750. The Horse Guards (1742), Holkham (1734), and Devonshire House (1734) were designed by William Kent. S. Mary-le-Strand (1717), S. Martin's (1721), the Senate House, Cambridge (1730), and the Radcliffe Library, Oxford (1747) were by James Gibbs.

Somerset House (1776), by Sir William Chambers, is a typical example of late 18th century classic ; accurate in proportion, with refined details and excellent workmanship and materials. Chambers published his " Decorative Part of Civil Architecture " in 1759.

Other architects of this period were George Dance, the elder, who built the Mansion House, completed in 1753 ; Paine, Carr of York, Gandon, Dance the younger, and Robert and James Adam, who designed and built the Adelphi (1768) and many streets and mansions in London and Edinburgh. Robert Adam also designed many accessories, such as console tables and candelabra, and on the ceilings, pilasters, and panels were composition enrichments (plates 42 and 43).

Of modern Renascence, the Wellington Monument in S. Paul's Cathedral, by Alfred Stevens, is distinguished by its strong personality and architectonic treatment of composition, and the beauty and singular grace of its details.

TWO ORNAMENTAL PANELS FOR PAINTING, STUCCO, OR CARVING, BY MATTHEW DARLY.

RELIEF ORNAMENT FROM THE WEKALA. CAIRO
ARABIAN. 15TH CENTURY

2

CAPITAL FROM THE COURT OF
THE LIONS. ALHAMBRA

3

FRIEZE, IN MOSQUE OF SULTAN HASAN. CAIRO. 14TH CENTURY.
FROM THE ART OF THE SARACENS."

4

CEILING DECORATION, FROM
THE ALHAMBRA MORESQUE

6   7   8

WALL DECORATION FROM THE ALHAMBRA, SPAIN.   MORESQUE.

OHAMMEDAN ORNAMENT.

The rise and development of the Arabs is most remarkable: the wide appreciation and liberal patronage of the arts by the Khalifs; the influence of the Mohammedan religion and precepts upon contemporary and later periods of art; the distinct individuality and geometrical arrangement of their ornamentation; all had a most marked effect upon tradition and craftsmanship.

The history commences with Mohammed, A.D. 569-683, who founded and consolidated the empire, of which, under Omar, A.D. 635, Damascus became the capital; in A.D. 638 Kufa and Bassora were founded in Persia. In A.D. 641 Egypt was conquered, and the Mohammedan capital, Fustât, founded. Persia was conquered in A.D. 632, Spain invaded in A.D. 711, Bagdad in Persia became the capital of the Arabian Khalifs in A.D. 762, and in A.D. 827 Sicily was conquered; but it was not until the dynasty of Ibn-Tulun, A.D. 878-914, that the history of Cairene art begins, of which the mosque of Ibn-Tulun in Fustât, or old Cairo, is the earliest example. Under the Fatima dynasty, A.D. 867-1171, Cairo was founded, and the arts, receiving further encouragement, were now introduced into Sicily and Europe. In A.D. 711 the Mohammedan invasion of India took place. In A.D. 796-965 the mosque of Cordova was built, and in A.D. 1236 the kingdom of Grenada was founded and the Alhambra was built, by Mohammed ben Alhamar, A.D. 1248, and Mohammedan art, as exemplified in architectural decorations, arms and armour, woodwork, ivory, textile fabrics, and illuminated books, reached its culmination under the Mamluk dynasty, A.D. 1250-1516.

Thus the Arabs, from a roving tribe, became, by religious zeal and conquests, the most powerful and the wealthiest nation of mediæval times, assimilating and influencing the customs and the arts of the different nations and provinces.

The term MOHAMMEDAN ART includes ARABIAN, MORESQUE, PERSIAN, INDIAN, and SICILIAN, all having the same characteristics, yet distinguished by the racial influence and custom. The Arabian is marked by its flowing, interlacing, and symmetrical lines, geometrical arrangement (doubtless derived from Byzantine sources), and its prevalence of inscriptions or texts from the Koran. In Spain a more complex geometrical arrangement is found, intermingled with a flowing foliage or arabesque of a purely conventional type. This style is noticeable for its entire absence of any natural forms and its abundant use of inscriptions and glazed enamelled tiles, distinctly influenced by Persian tradition, though purely geometric and formal. These tiles cover the lower part of the wall, the upper portion, as also the ceiling, being decorated with arabesques of modelled plaster in flat relief, of two or more planes, enriched with red, blue, white, and gold; this is typical of the Moresque style. The Sicilian work is remarkable for its beautiful fabrics of silk and the prevalence in its ornament of birds, animals, and heraldic forms, showing the continuity of the traditions of Persia (plate 75 and page 160).

PLATE

SILICEOUS GLAZED EARTHENWARE RHODIAN, 15 & 16 Century,
WHITE GROUND. RED FLOWERS. BLUE & GREEN FOLIAGE.

HOOKER BASE. GLAZED EARTHENWARE WITH
MUSSEROUS ORNAMENT 16 OR 17 CENTURY.

EARTHENWARE PLATE 16 CENTURY.
BLUE GROUND. WHITE & GREEN FLOWERS & FOLIAGE.

BLUE WHITE & GREEN WALL TILES.

RHODIAN TILE. WHITE ORNAMENT ON RED GROUND, THE DARK PART DEEP BLUE
15 OR 16 CENTURY.

TILE FROM CAIRO. RHODIAN, 16 CENTURY. BLUE GROUND.

BLUE AND GREEN TILE. FROM DAMASCUS.

(1) PORTION OF A CARPET FROM THE MOSQUE AT ARDEBIL, PERSIA. 1540 A.D.

(2) PORTION OF A 16TH CENTURY PERSIAN CARPET.

(3) PORTION OF EMBROIDERED BEDSPREAD, SOUTH INDIAN, EARLY 18TH CENTURY.

ERSIAN ORNAMENT.

The early art of Persia was similar to that of Assyria and Babylon, having the same forms, materials, and traditions. With the accession of the Sassanides, A.D. 223, came the introduction of the elliptical dome, so typical of eastern architecture. This dome rested on pendentives, which occupied the angles of the square base. These pendentives and the elliptical dome are distinctive features in Mohammedan architecture.

The industrial arts of Persia were largely influenced by the traditional arts of Assyria and Chaldea. This tradition was carried on with rare skill and selective power by the Persians, culminating in the splendid period of Shah Abbas, A.D. 1586-1625. The vitality, beauty, and interest of detail, combined with perfect decorative adaptation to material, are characteristic of the textiles, pottery, metal work, and illuminated manuscripts of the 15th, 16th, and 17th centuries.

The Mohammedan conquest of Persia, A.D. 632-637, by Abu Bekr, the successor of Mohammed, largely influenced the development of the arts of the Persians, who adopted the customs and habits of contemporary races, yet preserved all the characteristics of their art; and there is no doubt that the art of the Arabs was founded upon the traditional arts of Persia.

Persian decoration is characterized by a fine feeling for form and colour, and for the singularly frank renderings of natural plants, such as the pink, hyacinth, tulip, rose, iris, and the pine and date. These are used with perfect sincerity and frankness, and are essentially

PERSIAN
PLATE. 16TH
CENTURY. S.K.M.

89

decorative in treatment, combining harmony of composition of mass, beauty of form, and purity of colour. It was doubtless owing to these qualities, together with the perfect adaptation of ornament to material, that the Persian style so largely influenced contemporary work, and especially the European textile fabrics of the 16th and 17th centuries. The illustrations given are of some familiar types of Persian adaptations of natural flowers, doubtless chosen for their significance, beauty of growth and form, and appropriateness of decorative treatment. Purely Arabian forms, as given in plate 44, are frequently associated with the Persian floral treatment, showing the influence of the artists of Damascus. Many fine examples of lustred wall tiles, dating from the 10th and 11th centuries, are in the Victoria and Albert Museum, South Kensington, of which the blue, brown, and turquoise colouring is of a splendid quality. They often have Arabic inscriptions interspersed with the floral enrichments, as in plate 48 (5). Examples of wall tiles of the 8th century have been found in the ruins of Rhages.

These lustred tiles (v. below) are a remarkable instance of tradition or hereditary proclivity. This art, beginning with the enamelled bricks of Babylon, and the later frieze of Susa (page 19) with its brilliant enamel and fine colour, was continued by the Persians, and, passing to the Arabs, the tradition was carried to Cairo, Spain, and Majorca ; thence into Italy, where enamelled lustre ware was made, differing from the original Persian in its frequent absence of utility, which was fundamental to the art of the Persians.

While Indian ornament has a conventional rendering of plants, and the introduction of the lion, tiger, and the elephant (fig. 2, plate 49), in Persian work there is a still less formal constructive arrangement, with floral forms clearly defined in line and mass, and the introduction of the human figure with the horse, the lion, the tiger, and birds (plate 46 (2)). In Persian carpets, animal forms, chosen with rare selective power and judgment, are combined with the typical floral enrichment of Persia, with a wealth of colour, admirable detail of spacing and mass, beauty of incident and vigour, and appropriateness of treatment (plate 46 (1), 47, 48, figs. 1 and 4). These are features that distinguish the industrial designs of Persia, and it is doubtless due to the interest and vitality of their ornament that we owe the remarkable influence of Persian art upon the contemporary and later craftsmanship of Europe.

STAR-SHAPED PERSIAN LUSTRED TILES.

Plate 47.

A PERSIAN RUG, OF ABOUT 1600.

1

2

3

WHITE PATTERN ON RED GROUND.
GENOSE FROM A PERSIAN DESIGN. S.K.M

4

FROM A PERSIAN DRAWING
SOUTH KENSINGTON MUSEUM

VELVET STUFF WITH
RAISED PATTERN OF VASES,
FLOWERS & FIR CONES IN
CRIMSON & GREEN, ON A
WHITE GROUND
ITALIAN (GENOSE)
FROM A PERSIAN
DESIGN 16 TH Century
SOUTH KENSINGTON
MUSEUM

5

PORTION OF PERSIAN
CARPET
SOUTH KENSINGTON
MUSEUM

PANEL OF TILES FROM THE SENARIYEH MOSQUE AT DAMASCUS. 1580.   SOUTH KENSINGTON MUSEUM
TILES 6¼ INCHES SQUARE

1
2
WOVEN FABRIC.
BENARES. S.K.M.

COLUMN FROM
TEMPLE OF VISHA.
BENARES.

3

PRINTED COTTON. BOCK COLLECTION.
MANCHESTER.

4

6

SILK BROCADE. WITH PINE SHAPED
FLOWERS. BENARES. S.K.M.

5

COTTON PRINT. WITH FLOWERS IN
THE FORM OF A LEAF. S.K.M.

6

CASHMERE SCARF. WITH THE PATTERN
FORMED OF PINES. SCARLET GROUND. S.K.M.

INDIAN ORNAMENT.

The civilization of India dates from the remote past, but the oldest remains of its art and architecture are connected with the Buddhist religion, introduced by the prophet Sakya Muni (638 B.C.). This influenced the arts of India till A.D. 250, when the Jaina style was adopted. The examples of Buddhist architecture consist of Topes (which were sacred or monumental temples, either detached or rock-cut), and monasteries. The rock-cut temples usually consist of a nave and aisles, and a semi-circular recess containing a statue of the seated Buddha. The hall has square or octagonal columns, with bracket capitals (fig. 1). The finest examples of these temples are those at Ajanta, which are richly decorated in colour with incidents of Hindoo mythology. The fine temples at Ellora, which are cut entirely out from the rock, are of the Jaina period (A.D. 250). The pagodas at Chedombaram are of the Brahmin period, as is also the great hall of 1,000 pillars, which is 190 by 340 ft., containing the sacred image of the god Siva.

Alexander the Great conquered India 327 B.C., and doubtless left the influence of the Persian tradition in India. This influence was still further developed by the commercial intercourse of Persia and India, and by the Arabian invasion of India in A.D. 711, when a Mohammedan dynasty was established (711-1152). This largely controlled and influenced the arts under the Mogul dynasty (1525-1857), when the decorative arts and the manufacture of the beautiful woven brocades and silks were fully developed. The splendid carpets and rugs, printed cottons, metal work, and fine enamels of this dynasty bear a remarkable tribute to the vitality, originality of ideas, and the practical utility of the industrial arts of India.

Indian ornament has the typical Mohammedan division of spaces, but is more flowing and graceful than the pure Arabian style. These divisions are filled with fine conventional floral forms, such as the lotus, the date or hom, the iris, the rosette, and the pine. This pine is treated occasionally as a single flower, but more frequently as a cluster of flowers, which still retains the distinctive form of the pine (plate 49, figs. 2, 4, and 6).

Typical also of this period is the judicious treatment of the elephant, lion, tiger, peacock, and the human figure, as accessories in the decorative arts of India. They were applied with rare knowledge and skill, combined with an artistic perception of applied art, and show a very strong affinity with contemporary Persian ornament (plate 46 (3)).

Indian ornament has a more conventional rendering of natural forms than the frank treatment of Persian ornament. Block printing upon silk and cotton fabrics reached a high degree of perfection during the last century. The inventiveness and significance of detail, the charm of composition of line and mass, and the beautiful colour of these printed fabrics, are a reflex of the decorative feeling for beauty by the people of India.

WOVEN SILK. CHINESE. 18TH CENTURY.
1

WOVEN SILK. CHINESE. 18TH CENTURY
BOCK COLLECTION. MANCHESTER

BOCK COLLECTION.
MANCHESTER

4 CHINESE DRAGON.

3
CHINESE
DRAGON.
EMBROIDERY.

PAINTED BORDERS. MING DYNASTY. A.D 1338.

PAINTED PORCELAIN, 15TH CENTURY

94

(3) PRINTED COTTON HANGING, EARLY 19TH CENT. JAVANESE, SHOWING CHINESE INFLUENCE.

(2) EMBROIDERED WALL HANGING, 16TH CENTURY.

(1) PART OF EMBROIDERED SILK COVERLET, 19TH CENTURY.

CHINESE ORNAMENT.

The early bronzes, enamels, porcelain, and textile fabrics of China are indicative of the perfection and luxuriance of the decorative arts of that ancient empire. This perfection is shown by a splendid technique and a fine appreciation of colour and ornamentation, differentiated from the western nations by myths, traditions, and the remarkable persistency of a few typical forms through many centuries, doubtless owing to the profound ancestral worship and veneration for the past. The dragon was represented under many aspects, frequently forming vigorous lines of composition (plate 51, figs. 3, 4). The beautiful flora of the country largely influenced Chinese art. The peony and chrysanthemum (frequently highly conventionalized) are typical examples, forming the elements of decorative design. Geometric forms, such as the hexagon, octagon, and the circle, enriched with flowers or the fret, are largely used. The many splendid examples of bells, gongs, and incense-burners in bronze and iron ; the carvings in wood, ivory, and jade ; the beautiful woven silks, richly patterned with the conventional chrysanthemum, the peony (fig. 2), or with geometrical forms, filled with the fret or rosettes (fig. 1) ; the magnificent fabrics, designed with dragons, birds, and conventional flowers, excellent in technique and colour (frontispiece) ; and the richness and purity of their porcelain, more especially the old blue and white of the Ming dynasty, A.D. 1568-1640 (plate 50, fig. 4), all testify to the versatility and vitality of the Chinese decorative arts in the past.

Their architecture was distinguished by complexity and quaintness of form, rather than beauty of proportion and detail. Their pagodas and temples, of which numerous examples are still extant, were of wood, iron, brick, or marble ; and one, the Nanking Pagoda, A.D. 1412-31, destroyed in 1854, was encased with yellow and green porcelain tiles, and had 150 bells pendant from the roof. Pagodas are from 3 to 13 storeys in height ; that at Peking has 13 storeys and is 275 ft. high, the Nanking porcelain pagoda was 250 ft. high, and a fine brick one of 7 storeys on the River Yangtsze is 140 ft. in height. The roof of each storey curves outwards and upwards, and usually supports a balcony.

Colour symbolism is an important feature of all Chinese art, especially that associated with their religious rites.

In the Temple of Heaven during the religious ceremonies blue is the prevailing colour ; blue light is transmitted into the building, the sacrificial vessels are of blue porcelain, the robes of the priests are of blue brocades, and the exterior is covered with tiles of a deep cobalt blue. Yellow porcelain and brocades are used in the Temple of Earth, red in the Temple of the Sun, and white in that of the Moon.

CRANES.
PAINTED BY MORI IPPO,
1840. BRITISH MUSEUM.

THE QUICK POSTMAN, FROM THE MANGWA,
OR ROUGH SKETCHES, BY HOKUSAI. 1760-1849.

WOVEN SILKS.

THE KIRI-MON & KIKU IMPERIAL CRESTS.

APANESE ORNAMENT.

The arts of Japan, though doubtless owing their origin to China, are differentiated by a keener observation of nature and a more literal treatment of landscape, bird, and animal life, and the beautiful flora of the country—the " kiku " or chrysanthemum, the " botan " or peony, the " kosai " or iris, the " yuri " or lily, the " kiri " or paulawina imperialis (somewhat resembling our horse chestnut), the " matsu " or fir, and the " take " or bamboo—likewise the peacock, the crane, the duck, the pheasant, and many smaller beautiful birds, together with reptiles, insects, and fishes ; all are elements in the decorative arts, being rendered with remarkable fidelity and delicacy of touch, united with a fine feeling for composition of line.

Physical phenomena, such as the snow-clad mountain, Fujiyama, have always exercised considerable influence upon the Japanese mind. This may be readily seen in the thirty colour prints by Hiroshige, and the hundred views of this mountain by Hokusai. The cherry and plum blossoms, emblems of the beauty and purity of spring, are also intimately associated with the life and the ornament of the people. It is this literal treatment of natural types, the marvellous technique, and especially the significance of the forms chosen, that constitutes the charm of the earlier Japanese art. It is singular that the materials used by the Japanese should be of little intrinsic value. Having no jewellery, they use little of the precious metals ; iron, bronze, enamels, clay, wood, and lac being the chief materials utilized in the decorative arts of Japan. Bronze is one of the earliest materials used in the arts of Japan, and their large statue of Buddha at Kamakura, cast in A.D. 748, rests upon a lotus flower with fifty-six petals, 10 ft. by 6 ft., and the height from base to top of figure is 63 ft.

Pottery made but little development until the 13th century, when a coloured earthenware, having but little decoration, was produced at Seto, in Owari, and it was not until 1513 that porcelain was introduced from China into Arita, by Shondzui ; and at the commencement of the 17th century a fine porcelain, decorated with birds and flowers in blue, red, and gold, now known as " Old Japan " or " Old Hizen," was produced. Kioto, Seto, and Arita were also noted for the production of a fine blue-and-white porcelain.

Cloisonné enamels, introduced in the 17th century, reached a high degree of technical excellence, but never quite reached the beauty, purity, and harmony of colour that characterized the old Chinese cloisonné.

Lacquer developed in Japan during the Heian period (A.D. 782-1192). The Ashikaga period (A.D. 1336-1573) saw the rise and progress of lacquer decoration in relief ; and in the Tokugarva period (1615-1867) the technical skill of the craftsmen reached a high water mark. Towards the middle years of the 18th century an abundance of detail overwhelmed the old simplicity of motif.

THE ARCHITECTURAL CAPITAL.

The form and enrichment of the Architectural Capital offer one of the most interesting and instructive fields of study in the history and evolution of architecture and ornament. The remarkable persistency of the capital as a distinctive feature in architecture may be traced through many centuries, though differentiated by climatic conditions and racial influences, yet still preserving a remarkable similarity of form and enrichment among the various nations of the earth.

The function of the capital is to sustain and transmit to the columns the weight of the entablature or archivolt, and the beauty and appropriateness of the capital depends (1) upon this functional treatment of strength ; (2) upon the beauty of profile or mass ; (3) upon the enrichment and proportion of the capital.

The dignified Doric capital of the Greeks illustrates these functions and conditions by its perfect adaptability, simple functional strength, beauty of profile, appropriateness of enrichment and proportion and harmony of parts, qualities which are essential to beauty of architecture. In the Parthenon (438 B.C.), we have the finest treatment of this capital—a treatment full of dignity, reserve, and unison of profile (plate 6). The many examples of the Doric Order in Greece and her colonies attest to the esteem in which this order was held by the Greeks. The Indian capital (plate 49) exhibits the same functional treatment by the use of brackets or modillions, which undoubtedly are a survival of a wooden construction, and which are typical of Eastern architecture.

The remarkable persistency of the profile and enrichment of the capital extending through a period of 4,000 years may be illustrated by a series of diagrams of typical examples. The profile of the capital has not varied to any appreciable extent in the examples here given, and the enrichment of the bell is remarkable for its persistency, though

EGYPT-
IAN CAP-
ITAL FROM
PHILÆ.

differentiated by racial influences. The Corinthian capital, with its volutes and acanthus foliage, is but the architectural continuity of the Egyptian capital. The only pure Greek example of this order is from the monument of Lysicrates, but the Romans continued the tradition, assimilating and elaborating until they produced the magnificent capitals of the portico of the Pantheon and the temple of Castor and Pollux. In these examples the leaves are arranged in series of two rows of eight leaves each, the volutes springing from sheaths and stems between the leaves which support the angle of the volutes. The example of early French Gothic has similar characteristics and illustrates the continuity of style.

The Ionic capital (page 13), though one of the most persistent in the history of architecture, never reached the architectonic perfection of other capitals. There is a want of unity between the volutes and ovolo of the capital; in brief, it has neither coherence nor harmony of parts. The exquisite craftsmanship of the capitals of the Erechtheum, with their anthemion enrichment of the greatest purity, the beauty of the ovolo and the subtility of the volutes compensates to some extent for the lack of unison (plate 6). The enrichment of the architectural capital is no doubt a survival of the primitive custom of

binding floral forms round the simple functional capital, these forms being afterwards perpetuated in stone or marble.

In early Corinthian examples these floral forms were frequently of beaten metal, which, in turn, gave place to the beautiful marble foliage of the Greeks and Romans.

That the ancients used metal work in their capitals we have abundant proof.

The Composite capital is deficient in coherence and unity of parts,

having the same defects as its prototype the Ionic. The annexed illustration gives an unusual treatment by the introduction of the human figure in the centre of the face of the capital.

The Byzantine capital differs from those of the Greeks and Romans in its marked symbolism of detail and the prevalence of the cushion form. Functionally, this type of capital is admirable, yet it lacks the vigorous upward growth of the Egyptian and early Gothic capitals.

The Byzantine capitals have a wonderful complexity and variety of detail, such as interlacing circles and crosses with their symbolism, basket work, chequered details, and the traditional sharp acanthus foliage of the Greeks.

These features are seen in the greatest profusion at S. Sofia at Constantinople ; S. Apollinare and S. Vitale at Ravenna, and S. Marco at Venice. These splendid capitals of a splendid period are exceedingly beautiful in fertile inventiveness of enrichment, and show the assimilative power of the Byzantine craftsmen. The abundant use of chequer work, wreaths of chain work and of lily work in Byzantine capitals, many of which are figured in Ruskin's "Stones of Venice," show the continuity of style and tradition in architecture.

The Byzantine capitals have the square abacus, usually consisting of a simple fillet and chamfer enriched with the billet, dentil or star pattern. The Dosseret, a singular adjunct to the capital, was introduced during this period ; it was a cushion-shaped or cubical stone placed upon the abacus of the capital to give additional height.

The Byzantine influence is seen upon the Norman capitals with their square abacus of fillet and chamfer, and the cushion profile of capital. Some remarkable Siculo-Norman capitals are in the cloisters of the Benedictine Monastery of Monreale in Sicily (A.D. 1174-1184). The great fertility of inventiveness in the 200 capitals, their storiation, the intermingling of figures, birds, and animals with the classic and Byzantine foliage makes this cloister one of the most remarkable in the history of the world. The Arabian capital, which frequently shows the traditional volute, differs from the typical bell-shaped form in its marked squareness of profile with flat or low reliefs enriched with colour.

The early Gothic capital is one of the most vigorous and beautiful.

The perfect adaptability of its foliage to stone carving, the rich-

ness of its detail, the spiral growth of its foliage, and the vigorous contrast of light and shade are the chief character-istics of this period. Lack-ing, perhaps, the delicacy or variety of detail of the Byzantine period, or the later Gothic work, it excelled them in the appropriateness of its enrichment, which is more beautiful in the early English examples with their circular abacus than in contemporary French capitals where the square abacus was prevalent. The transition from the cir-cular column to the square abacus was always felt to be a difficulty, and was rarely overcome, but in the circular abacus of the early English capitals we have a break in the continuity of the style of the capital.

CAPITALS
FROM THE
CLOISTERS
of MONREALE

The English foliage of this period differs from the French in the use of a deep mid-rib and simple trefoil leaf. The French

EARLY
ENGLISH
CAPITAL.
ELY
CATHE-
-DRAL.

ARABIAN
CAPITAL
FROM THE
ALHAMBRA

examples have a less pronounced mid-rib, and the leaf is convex in form and divided into three lobes, and the foliage adheres more closely to the bell, consequently the brilliant play of light and shade which is so characteristic of early English work, is generally absent from French examples (fig. 12, plate 21).

The decorated Gothic capitals differ essentially from those of the early Gothic period, a more natural type of foliage being used, consisting of the briony, maple, mallow, and oak. This foliage was

SOUTH- DECO-
WELL RATED
MINSTER CAPITAL

carved with singular delicacy of touch and grace of profile, and is beautiful in its modelling and play of light and shade, yet frequently the capitals are trivial in conception and arrangement, lacking that architechtonic character which is so essential to all architectural constructive features.

The perpendicular, or late Gothic capital, was usually octagonal in form with square conventional foliage of the vine, showing a marked decadence in tradition and craftsmanship.

14TH CENTURY
CAPITAL
CHARTRES.

The Renascence capital was frequently marked by a fine feeling for profile, splendid craftsmanship, diversity of enrichment, and vitality of conception, more especially in Italy.

RENASCENCE
CAPITAL
VENICE.

ART II.

The Applied Arts.

WOODCUT FROM THE GROTESQUE ALPHABET OF 1464
(FLEMISH), BRITISH MUSEUM.

ENGRAVED PANEL BY HEINRICH ALDEGREVER, ONE OF THE
LITTLE MASTERS OF GERMANY.

BYZANTINE WALL MOSAIC COLOURED ORNAMENT on GOLD GROUND. S.T MARK'S VENICE

ROMAN PAVEMENT. 2.ND CENTURY. VATICAN ROME

WALL MOSAIC OF COLOURED MARBLES ARABIAN. 14.TH CENTURY. S.K.M.

MOSAIC FLOOR. ROMAN. FOUND AT ROME.

MARBLE INLAY. ITALIAN. 15.TH CENTURY CHURCH OF S.T JACOPO. FLORENCE

ROMAN PAVEMENT IN RED, WHITE & BLACK MARBLE FOUND IN 1795. NEAR LINCOLN

MOSAICS.

Mosaic is the art of forming patterns by means of pieces of variously-coloured materials fitted together, and is broadly divided into *Opus Tesselatum*, of small cubes, like dice ; *Opus Sectile,* of slices of marble ; and *Opus Musivum,* or glass mosaic : and may be subdivided into *Opus Figinum,* or ceramic mosaic ; *Opus Vermiculatum,* with (a) *majus,* black and white marble ; (b) *medium,* all materials and colours ; and (c) *minus,* of minute tesserae, used for furniture inlay. *Opus Alexandrinum* is an inlay of porphyry and serpentine on white marble.

It was in Rome that the art of mosaic was brought to its greatest perfection. The finest example is from the House of the Faun, Pompeii, and represents the battle of Issus, between Alexander and Darius. This mosaic, of the 3rd century B.C., is probably a copy of a Greek painting. A good example of this period is the so-called " Pliny's Doves," a representation of four doves upon a basin.

Many fine Roman mosaics have been found in England, at Cirencester, London, Lincoln (*v.* plate), Leicester, and at Brading.

Magnificent examples of mosaic are found at Ravenna and Constantinople, reaching a culmination at Venice. Of the Ravenna mosaics (page 33), those of the Baptistery, A.D. 450, S. Apollinare and S. Vitale are typical examples of the earlier Byzantine mosaics, having dark green and blue backgrounds, with tesserae about ⅜ in. square. The beautiful frieze of male and female saints in S. Apollinare extends along both sides of the nave, and is 10 ft. high. The vaulting and domes of S. Mark are entirely covered with the characteristic 11th century Byzantine gold ground mosaic, formed by fusing two pieces of glass together with gold leaf between. At Santa Sophia, Constantinople, and in the Capella Palatina, Palermo, are other fine mosaics.

Splendid examples of *Opus Alexandrinum* are found on the pavement of the Pantheon, Rome (A.D. 118-38). Other examples, dating from the 8th century, are in Rome, in the nave of the Basilica of San Lorenzo fuori le Mure, having interlacing circular bands of geometrical mosaic on white marble. In Santa Maria in Trastevere, the pattern is formed of hexagons and stars of six or eight points. A beautiful design of a large eight-pointed star of porphyry, with the triangles between the points of the star filled with small geometric mosaic, is in the Church of S. S. Giovanni e Paolo.

In the 13th and 14th centuries in Italy, the Cosmati (a family of mosaicists) produced some geometrical inlaid mosaics upon the vertical and twisted pillars in the cloisters of San Giovanni Laterano, and on the splendid " Ambone," or pulpit, in Santa Maria in Araceli, Rome. On the tombs of Edward (A.D. 1270) and Henry III. (1280), in Westminster Abbey, are some good examples of this " Cosmati " mosaic.

TYPICAL FORMS OF GREEK VASES

HYDRIA. FOR CARRYING WATER.

CRATER. FOR MIXING WINE AND WATER.

CANTHAROS. WINE CUP.

AMPHORA. FOR CARRYING WINE

OINOCHOE. FOR POURING WINE.

LEKYTHOS. FOR POURING OIL.

KYLIX. WINE CUP.

No 2.3.4. 5 6 & 7 FROM THE MANCHESTER COLLECTION.

DANCING FIGURES FROM AN AMPHORA. B.C. 400.

2

OINOCHOE. B.C. 600.

3

TWO-HANDLED VASE. OEDIPUS. JOCASTA. AND THE SPHINX. B.C. 400. RED FIGURED PERIOD.

4

OINOCHOE, OR WATER JUG. B.C. 500.

5

AMPHORA. BLACK FIGURED PERIOD. B.C. 500.

6

LEKYTHOS RED FIGURED PERIOD.

7

RED FIGURED PERIOD.

KYLIX B.C. 400.

GREEK CERAMICS.

It is difficult in modern times to realise the importance of vases in ancient times. To the Greeks a vase was a receptacle for food or liquid, and was used for the adornment of the home ; it was used in the daily life of the living, and buried with the dead. Most of the finer vases found in Etruscan tombs are of Greek workmanship, imported from Greece or Grecian colonies ; some black unglazed Etruscan vases have been found, but painted vases of Etruscan origin are rare.

Early Greek pottery, dating probably from the 10th century, B.C., has been found in Greece, the colonies of Rhodes, Cyrene in Africa, and Naucratis in the delta of Egypt. These, showing a historic development, are arranged in groups, each with its distinctive characteristic. (1st) PRIMITIVE VASES, simple in shape, handles small or absent, decorations in simple line, punctured or incised, or in raised slip. (2nd) MYCENÆ or COLONIAL (900-700 B.C.) vases, often covered with a creamy slip, the designs, painted in brown and black, being derived from geometric patterns with marine and animal forms. (3rd) DIPYLON or GEOMETRIC (700 B.C.), with fret pattern enrichment, and panels with rude figures of men and animals in black and brown. (4th) PHALERON WARE (700-550 B.C.), with continuous bands of animals, probably derived from Phœnicia or Assyria (fig 4). Among the animals depicted, are placed portions of the fret pattern, a survival of the previous style. The details are incised through the black or brown figure, showing the colour of the clay body. A development of this Phaleron ware was the introduction of the rosette, taking the place of the fret pattern between the figures or the animals. (5th) BLACK FIGURE PERIOD (600-480 B.C.) vases, fine in profile, and with good handles, the body of the vase, in red ware, being painted with subjects of Grecian mythology in black, and the details incised ; the faces, arms, and legs of the female figures were afterwards painted in white or red slip and fired at a lower heat. The AMPHORA (fig. 5) was the chief form of this black figure period. Some fine examples are signed by Exekias and Amasis. (6th) THE TRANSITIONAL PERIOD (500-470 B.C.), when the black silhouette figures on a red ground gave way to the RED FIGURE PERIOD on a black ground. Artists of this style were Epiktetos, Pamphæios, Nicosthenes (page 21), and Pythos. Many of the vases by Nicosthenes resemble contemporary metal work in their shape and handles. The 7th group (525-400 B.C.) was the culminating period of Greek vase painting, the chief form employed being the KYLIX. A fine series of these *Kylikes*, with red figures on a black ground, signed by Cachrylion, Euphronios, Duris, Pethenos, and Hieron, are in the British Museum.

The later vases (400-200 B.C.) are the polychrome sepulchral " Lekythi," covered with white slip, and enriched with paintings, and the elaborate vases, decorated with subjects from the Greek drama, which were produced in the Greek cities of southern Italy.

1 ROMAN: RED LUSTROUS, OR SAMIAN WARE: WITH ENRICHMENTS

2 IN RELIEF, OBTAINED BY PRESSING INTO MOULDS & BY THE USE OF DIES. MUSEUM OF GEOLOGY.

3 ROMAN ORNAMENTED WITH PIPECLAY SLIP, ON BLACK GROUND. MUSEUM OF GEOLOGY.

5 A PORTION OF OIRON POTTERY. INLAY OF COLOURED CLAYS, ON THE WHITE BODY OF THE WARE

4 CHINESE VASE PAINTED WITH CHRYSANTHEMUMS & FOLIAGE in BLUE. MING DYNASTY. SOUTH KENSINGTON MUSEUM.

6 CANDLESTICK. OIRON. OR "HENRI-DEUX" WARE. A.D. 1524-40. S.K.M.

7 JARDINIÈRE. ROUEN WARE 1720 A.D. S.K.M.

8 PORCELAIN VASE. SEVRES. PERIOD OF LOUIS XVI. S.K.M.

9 I·THOMAS·TOFT

DISH OF SLIP WARE. BY THOMAS TOFT 1660. M of G.

10 WHITE GREEN & LILAC JASPER WEDGWOOD WARE. S.K.M.

11 MELEAGER. FULHAM STONEWARE BY DWIGHT. 1671-1700. BRITISH MUSEUM.

CERAMICS.

The antiquity of ceramic art and its scientific and artistic qualities, render this subject one of considerable interest to art students.

The plasticity of clay and its hardening qualities under the influence of intense heat, its adaptability to the most refined forms, its affinity for the beautiful glazes and enamels so often associated with pottery, and its splendid traditions of craftsmanship, of colour, form, and decorations, so beautiful and varied in character, all combine to invest the subject with a charm and fascination of its own. Intrinsically valueless in its natural state, it is capable of being rendered almost priceless by scientific workmanship and artistic skill. The history of this material, and of its easy adaptation to the most refined and intricate, as well as the simplest of forms, affords invaluable lessons for present-day students.

Pottery clay may be classified under three divisions or headings :— (1) EARTHENWARE, (2) STONEWARE, (3) PORCELAIN. Under the first are grouped the largest number of ceramic wares. The pottery of Egypt, the faience of Assyria and Persia, the Greek and Etruscan vases, the famous red ware from the Isle of Samoa, and its counterpart the Roman Samian ware, the beautiful Maiolica of Spain and Italy, and the Rouen, S. Porchaire, Delft, and most of our English pottery are earthenwares ; the paste or body consists of natural clays selected for their plasticity, their hardening qualities, their fusibility or their colour, which when burnt have a porous opaque body, usually dull in colour. This dulness was usually overcome by coating the ware with a slip of fine white clay, which, whilst not possessing inherent qualities to form pottery by itself, would adhere to the coarser coloured body of the earthenware, thereby forming a smooth white ground. The early Greek vases of Naucratis, the later Lekythos of the Greeks, the faience of Persia, the Mezza Maiolica and the Sgraffito of the early Italian Renascence, and our English slip ware are examples of this method of giving a smooth white surface to coarse coloured earthenware. A similar result to the slip covering was also produced by the use of a silicious glaze, rendered white and opaque by the addition of oxide of tin. Early Assyrian faience, Della Robbia ware, the Maiolica of Spain and Italy, and the wares of Delft and Rouen are earthenwares coated with a tin enamel.

The silicious glaze here referred to is prepared by fusing silicious materials with soda or potash, and is known as Vitreous, or glass glaze. Plumbeous, or lead glaze, is produced by the addition of oxide of lead to the silicious glaze, rendering it more fusible, and still transparent. A white opaque enamel formed by using oxide of tin with the vitreous glaze is termed Stanniferous, or tin enamel. These different processes of covering the porous body of the earthenware largely influenced the decorations and scheme of colouring. The beautiful faïence of Damascus and Rhodes is covered with the silicious slip or glaze, and painted with rich blues produced by cobalt, turquoise and green by cobalt and copper, and purple by the use of manganese, and then covered with an alkaline glaze.

In the Rhodian ware the same scheme of colour prevails, except that the purple is replaced by a fine opaque red of great body, called Rhodian red, produced from Armenian bole. On the Italian Maiolica, with its tin enamel and plumbeous glaze, there are fine blue, turquoise and green, but red is very poor in colour, and is generally replaced by rich yellow from antimony, and orange from iron. This white tin enamel was undoubtedly introduced into Europe by the Moors, as some tiles in the Alhambra date from 1273-1302.

A large number of bowls and dishes, known as Samian ware, but now called *Terra Sigillata* (seal clay), of Roman importation have been found in England. The paste is usually of a fine sealing-wax red, with a good glaze. These bowls are enriched with a series of horizontal bands, containing the festoon, the scroll, birds, animals, and figures. The bands, or friezes, are often divided by the traditional egg and tongue moulding (fig. 2). Clay moulds, impressed with stamps, were made and then fired. The red paste having been pressed into the mould, the interior was smoothly turned in the lathe. A mould of this character was found at York in 1874, so it is possible that some of this ware was made in England, by Roman potters. Roman pottery has also been found at Castor, near Peterborough, doubtless made at the former place, kilns for firing having been found on the same site. This Castor ware is usually brown, with a black glaze being ornamented with indented tool marks and raised slip patterns of pipeclay (fig. 3). Many Roman dishes and vases of a dark grey colour, ornamented with incised lines and raised bosses of clay have been found in the Upchurch Marshes in Kent. Little artistic pottery of the mediæval period, however, is known to exist. Early in the 13th century beautiful encaustic tiles were made for the great monasteries, abbeys, and cathedrals.

About 1500, the production of tiles was introduced into Holland, quantities of small blue and white ones, decorated with scriptural subjects, being made at Delft, and thence exported to England for the lining of fireplaces, etc. Some fine painted tiles or *Azulejos* were made at Valencia about the 17th century.

In the 16th century, the porcelain of China was introduced into Europe by the Dutch and Portuguese traders, and much of the Delft and Rouen ware subsequently produced was in imitation of this oriental porcelain. "Delft" ware, which takes its name from the small town of that name in Holland, dates from A.D. 1500, and is a ceramic coated with stanniferous enamel, decorated with a full and liquid brush upon the absorbent enamel ground, and then glazed with a plumbeous glaze. Some of this Delft ware is very fine in quality, the cobalt blues under the glaze being remarkably soft and rich in colour. Early examples were decorated with historical subjects, often containing numerous figures, the middle period being notable for its imitation of Chinese porcelain, and the application of coloured enamels on coloured grounds. Vast quantities of this kind of ware were manufactured up to 1760, and exported to all parts of Europe. The production of Delft ware was first introduced into England at Lambeth by some Dutch potters in 1676, being subsequently extended to Fulham, Bristol, and Liverpool.

The use of stanniferous enamel was introduced into France by Girolama della Robbia, son of Andrea della Robbia, during the reign of Francis I., and in the second half of the 16th century several Italian potters followed in his track. Enamelled ware similar to the later productions of Urbino was made at Nevers, where also was produced a fine ware decorated with Persian *motifs* in yellow and blue. At Rouen, also, a fine earthenware covered with a tin enamel was manufactured, the decorations consisting of the lambrequins or scallop pattern, symmetrical in arrangement, and converging to the centre of the plate or

SÈVRES PORCELAIN VASE OF LOUIS XV PERIOD.
BRONZE MOUNTS BY THOMIRE

dish. The ornament was based upon Chinese examples, influenced by the contemporary woven fabrics of France. The decorations were usually in blue, and with overglaze painting, *i.e.*, after the white enamel was fired, finer and more delicate detail being obtained by this process, but at the cost of the purity and liquid softness of colour which is so characteristic of Delft and oriental underglaze painting.

III

In Rouen ware, the ground is generally white, but some fine examples at the Victoria and Albert Museum have a soft yellow ground, a rich Indian yellow being sometimes introduced with the blue decoration. It was under the directions of Louis Poterat (1673) that this most beautiful faience was perfected.

Bernard Palissy (*d*. 1590), by repeated experiments, discovered the stanniferous or tin enamel. His first productions were rustic dishes, elaborately decorated with carefully modelled fishes, reptiles, and plants or natural foliage, covered with an enamel of great brilliancy and purity, were the chief productions. The later pottery of Palissy consisted of saltcellars, inkstands, ewers, with elaborate figure decorations. An example of his work is seen on page 114.

Henri-Deux or S. Porchaire's ware (formerly described as Oiron ware) is of a pale straw colour, enriched with inlays of yellow, blue green, and brown coloured clays, the interlacing and arabesque ornamentation being similar in type to the contemporary bookbinding of Maioli and Grolier.

Many early examples of Staffordshire slip ware are to be found in England, consisting chiefly of candlesticks, cups, tygs, posset pots, piggins, and plates, the slip decorations being in yellow, white, and brown. This ware was made at Wrotham as early as 1649, and by Thomas Toft, at Shilton, about 1660 (fig. 9). Marbled, combed, and tortoise-shell ware were formed by using colour slips or clays. Agate and onyx ware were formed by layers of different coloured clays, crossed, cut, and pressed into moulds. These methods were perfected by Thomas Wheildon and Josiah Wedgwood, who perfected both the Queen's and the variegated ware. Queen's ware of a creamy colour was made chiefly for dinner and dessert services, being decorated with painted flowers in enamel.

In 1775, Wedgwood introduced his famous Jasper ware, and Jasper dip or washed Jasper. This latter ware was dipped into admixtures of metallic oxides, producing blue, lilac, pink, sage green, olive, yellow, and black as desired. The decorations in low relief are of the purest white (fig. 10), and in the traditional classic style, the figures being arranged as cameo medallions, or in bands with the scroll, the festoon, and the vine in delicate relief, *v*. figure, page 115. Many of these beautiful cameos were designed or modelled by Flaxman, Pacetti and Angelini, Bacon, Hackwood, Stothard, Tassie, and Webber.

STONEWARE differs from earthenware, owing to the presence of a larger percentage of silica in the plastic material, which, being fired at a greater degree of heat, vitrifies the body or paste into a kind of glass, thus ensuring a closeness and hardness of material not possessed by ordinary earthenware. Stoneware is usually glazed during the firing by throwing common salt into the kiln, which being volatilized, re-acts upon the silica in the body, forming with it a silicate of soda or glass, having a minute granular texture. The usefulness and the artistic character of stoneware was perfected by the Flemish and German potters of the 16th century.

The principal varieties of this ware are the grey and white " Canette " of Siegburg, near Bonn (see annexed fig. and plate 66), and the pale brown or grey ware of Raeren, near Aix-la-Chapelle, with its incised and stamped enrichments, sometimes with blue decoration. Frechen, near Cologne, probably supplied the " Bellarmines " or " Grey beards," largely imported into England under the name of " Cologne Pots." Examples of this Frechen ware were frequently ornamented with a raised scroll of oak leaves. Grenzhausen, in Nassau, produced a beautiful grey ware, having delicately moulded reliefs filled in with blue and purple. Many grey jugs ornamented with the initials of William III., Queen Anne, and George I., were imported into England from the Nassau kilns.

A stoneware similar to Rhenish stoneware, also termed by him " Cologne ware," was produced at Fulham by John Dwight, about 1685. Some fine jugs and a few cleverly modelled unglazed statuettes, believed to have been made at this place, are to be seen in the British Museum (fig. 11).

Another peculiar red stoneware, porcelain (or Red China as it was called) was made near Burslem by the brothers Elers (1688-1710), the ornamentation being obtained by pressing sharp intaglio copper moulds upon pieces of clay attached to the shaped ware. Astbury (1710-39), continued the traditions of Elers, producing a fine white stoneware, which largely influenced the Staffordshire pottery of that period. A stoneware was also made at Nottingham from 1700-1750.

PORCELAIN is technically known under the terms " hard paste " (" pâte dure ") and " soft " (" pâte tendre "). Hard porcelain is made from clays containing much alumina and felspar or decomposed granite, having but little plasticity, which necessarily influ- enced the shape or profile of the vessel. The beauty of form which is so typical of the

"CANETTE" OF WHITE STONE WARE, SIEGBURG, 1573.

Greek earthenware vase, is absent in porcelain, where the cylin- drical or octagonal form is principally used. " Pâte tendre " is a soft and vitreous porcelain, having a great affinity for the beautiful coloured glazes and enamels used in the early examples of Sèvres.

During the Ming dynasty in China (1568-1640), porcelain reached its highest development in the perfection of its body, ornamentation, colour and glazes, blue and turquoise being the chief colours of this period ; this limited range of colour was owing to the intense heat required to fuse the felspar glaze upon the hard porcelain.

Amongst the earliest known pieces brought from China to England are a couple of bowls given by Philip of Austria to Sir Thomas Trenchard in 1506. But whatever the date, it was inevitable that attempts should be made to imitate this beautiful ceramic. Florentine or Medician porcelain was made in 1575-80. It was not, however, until 1690 or 1700, that a similar manufacture was established at Rouen and S. Cloud. In 1709 Böttger commenced making hard porcelain at Meissen, in Saxony, subsequently producing some excellent examples about 1715. This was the commencement of the well-known Dresden china. In 1768, the manufacture of hard porcelain was adopted at Sèvres, replacing that of "pâte tendre" which had been in use from 1670. Both "pâte dure" and "pâte tendre" were made at Buen Retiro in Madrid (A.D. 1759), all the porcelain manufactured for the first twenty years being kept for the exclusive use of the Royal family. There are some finely modelled Buen Retiro tiles in the Royal Palace at Madrid.

About the middle of the 18th century the manufacture of porcelain was established in England. A factory at Bow dates from at least 1744, and in 1750 there was a factory working at Bristol. That of Worcester dates from the following year, while those of Derby, Longton Hall, and Lowestoft are more or less contemporary. The best examples of English porcelain of this period are copies of oriental porcelain, chiefly Persian and Chinese. A great advance in the technique of the porcelain produced in this country took place after the discovery of Kaolin in Cornwall, by William Cookworthy (1755). Of early English porcelains, those of Derby are, perhaps, the most refined

PLATE WITH THE CHILDHOOD OF BACCHUS, BY BERNARD PALISSY.

in form and in treatment of decoration, the plates, cups, and saucers having borders of blue or turquoise, with enrichments of festoons, leaves, and flowers ; many of the cups were pressed with fluted, ribbed, or imbricated patterns. The Derby works were in existence in 1750 ; in 1756 they were owned by William Duesbury and John Healy. In 1769 Duesbury purchased the Chelsea works and carried on the two simultaneously until 1784, when the Chelsea plant was transferred to Derby. From 1770-84 the ware called "Chelsea Derby" was produced, and between 1773-82 "Crown Derby" was introduced.

Porcelain of an excellent quality was made at Nantgarw between 1811-14, and at Swansea 1814-17, the decorations in enamel colours consisting of a natural rendering of flowers, birds, butterflies, and shells, chiefly painted by Richard Billingsley.

In some of the earlier Rockingham ware the outlines of the flowers and butterflies were in transfer printing, and the colouring was added by hand.

The earliest Worcester porcelain is often moulded with rococo reliefs, and painted within panels; and there are also a number of excellent pieces decorated in the Japanese style. About 1768 the factory engaged the best Chelsea painters and flourished until about 1780.

Transfer printing over the glaze was adopted at Worcester about 1757, the transfers being taken from copper plates engraved by Robert Hancock, a pupil of Ravenet, who was

A WEDGWOOD TEAPOT.

employed at the Battersea enamel works about 1750. Sadler and Green in 1756 also adopted over-glaze printing on the Liverpool delft. About 1770 under-glaze printing on the biscuit ware superseded the over-glaze process.

The Hispano-Moresque and Italian Maiolica (plate 57) are remarkable for the technical excellence of their white enamel, rich, blue, yellow, and orange, the iridescence of their gold and ruby lustre, and their high technical skill in painting.

ENGLISH EARTHENWARE of the 17th and 18th centuries, though traditional, showed a remarkable diversity in treatment and conception. The picturesque platter of the Toft school, with its quaint enrichment of trailing lines and heraldic forms in coloured slip, the fine red stoneware of Elers, with its graceful enrichments in delicate relief, and the varied and beautiful jasper ware of Wedgwood mark a distinct phase of the potter's art, and bear a tribute to the vitality and personality of the founders of the " *Potteries*."

SALTING COLLECTION.
S.K.M.

1

2

BLUE
GROUND
ORNAMENT
BUFF & ORANGE
CAFFAGGIOLO
WARE 1500

4

HISPANO-MORESQUE.
VALENCE 15TH CENTURY
BLUE INSCRIPTIONS, WITH
GOLDEN LUSTRED ORNAMENT.

3

5

PORTION OF BORDER OF A
MAIOLICA PLATE. ITALIAN 1550.
INCISED OR SGRAFFIATO ORNAMENT.
S.K.M.

A
PILGRIMS
BOTTLE. BY ORAZIO FONTANA.
URBINO WARE. 1530.
S.K.M.

6

PLATEAU FOR AN EWER.
BLUE ARABESQUES, ON ORANGE
GROUND. FAENZA. 1500.
S.K.M.

7

9

VASE BY
MAESTRO
GIORGIO.
GOLD & RUBY LUSTRE. S.K.M.

BOWL GUBBIO WARE. BY
MAESTRO GIORGIO.
1501
S.K.M.

8

10

DRUG
POT.
S.K.M. BOWL GUBBIO WARE.
PAINTED IN GRISAILLE. CASTEL DURANTE 1556. BY MAESTRO GIORGIO. S.K.M.

VASE 1530
CASTEL DURANTE WARE.
S.K.M.

MAIOLICA.

Maiolica or Italian faïence is an earthenware, coated with a stanniferous or tin glaze, termed enamel. This is formed by the addition of oxide of tin to a silicious glaze or slip, thus rendering it white and opaque, hence its name, enamel.

The origin of this beautiful ceramic art may be traced to Chaldea and Persia, with their magnificent enamelled bricks, such as the "Frieze of Archers" from the Palace of Susa (485 B.C.), and now in the Louvre (page 19). From Persia the art was carried by the Arabians to Fustat, or old Cairo, which was destroyed A.D. 1168, and amongst the ruins many fragments of gold or copper lustred ware have been found. This enamelled ware was introduced into Spain in the 13th century, and perfected there by the Moors, giving rise to the Hispano-Moresque ware. This ware was enriched with central heraldic arms, surrounded by concentric bands of foliage, arabesques, or inscriptions in blue, with a copper lustre. This Hispano-Moresque ware was manufactured chiefly at Malaga, Talavera, Triana, and Valencia, and dates from the Moorish occupation of Granada (A.D. 1235-1492).

In the Island of Majorca, from which this beautiful ware derives its name, fine examples were manufactured at an early date by Persian and Arabian potters. After the conquest of Majorca by the Pisans (A.D. 1115), many of these examples were introduced into Italy, the art being subsequently cultivated in some of the smaller central states.

The early Italian Maiolica was usually covered with a thin white "slip" or engobe of clay, which served as a ground for the coloured patterns. It was then coated with a lead glaze, and was known as mezza or mixed Maiolica. In some examples the design was scratched or engraved through the upper layer or white engobe, showing the darker body underneath. This type of ware, known as *sgraffito*, was also glazed with the lead glaze, forming, when fired, the beautiful iridescent lustre.

Few remains of a tin enamel of Italian workmanship have been found in Italy prior to the time of Luca della Robbia, who discovered an enamel of peculiar whiteness and excellence. The secret of its composition was kept by him, his nephew Andrea, and his great-nephews, Giovanni, Luca, and Girolamo, until 1507. The mezza Maiolica was then superseded by the true Maiolica, or the tin enamelled wares of Caffaggiolo, Castel Durante, Urbino, Pesaro. Faenza, Forli, Diruta, Siena, and Gubbio—cities all within a limited district, lying towards the east coast of Italy, and renowned centres of the Maiolica fabrication.

The Gubbio ware is noted for its metallic ruby and golden lustre, and was sometimes signed by Maestro Georgio (Georgio Andreoli), the finest period of this master was about 1525. The same artist also lustred many wares made by the potters of Urbino and Castel Durante. Other examples of Urbino ware are signed by Niccola da Urbino (1530) ; Orazio Fontana, the head of a noted family of potters, consisting of father, son, and grandson (1510-1600) ; Francesco Xanto Avelli (1530-40). Faenza ware was produced at the Casa Pirota Botega, and Siena ware was signed by Maestro Benedetto.

The chief characteristics of Caffaggiolo ware are arabesques and figures in white, grey, or yellow on a rich dark-blue ground. Urbino has small medallions with figures and blue and yellow arabesques on a white ground, called Raffaelesque, being from designs by Raffaelle del Colle. Faenza has a yellow ground with blue arabesques.

MAIOLICA VASE, ITALIAN,
c. 1570.

In brief, the number of colours that could be used on the absorbent tin enamelled ground with its lead glaze was somewhat limited, consisting of blue, turquoise, yellow, and orange. These colours are of great depth and translucency, and are only equalled by the blues and turquoise of China, Persia, and India.

Gubbio ware is frequently enriched with a raised curved fluting called *gadroons*, a most effective method of enhancing the beautiful ruby lustre of Maestro Giorgio. This Gubbio tradition was continued by Giorgio's son, Vicentio, called Maestro Cencio, and many beautiful lustre works are signed by him.

This lustre was produced by exposing the ware to the action of smoke during the firing in the kiln ; the smoke, being carbon in a highly-divided state, reduces the metallic salts of the pigment or glaze, forming a thin film of metal upon the surface, the beautiful iridescent lustre resulting from the relative thickness of the film.

Castel Durante was frequently enriched, on white or grey borders, with delicate raised scroll-work in white slip or enamel, a process called *Lavoro di sopra bianco* or *bianco sopra bianco*.

Faenza Maiolica has, frequently, the whole surface of the ground covered with a dark-blue enamel, enriched with dancing amorini and arabesques in blue, heightened with white *Sopra Azzurro*.

A frequent form of enrichment upon plates was to have small medallions painted with portraits and appropriate inscriptions, and doubtless intended as lovers' presents. They are known as *Amatorii Maiolica*.

TERRA COTTA.

Terra cotta is usually made from pure clay, which will burn to a white or yellow colour, or from impure, which will burn to a red colour owing to the presence of oxide of iron. Pure clay is a hydrous silicate of alumina, containing 47 parts per cent. of silica 40 of alumina, and 13 of water. Clay in this proportion is the Kaolin or china clay.

Fire clay, which is found in the coal measures, has a larger proportion of silica than Kaolin, and from it much of the terra cotta is made. When first dug out, it is hard and compact, and of a greenish-grey colour, deepening to black. It is often weathered before using; this causes it to "fall," and facilitates grinding. Old fire-clay, previously burnt ("grog" as it is called), is added to the new clay to counteract the excessive shrinkage to which all close-grained clays are liable.

The coarser the clay, the less the shrinkage. Pure clay contracts as much as one-eighth from the size of the mould: one-half of this contraction takes place in drying, the other half in burning.

The colour of the clay varies according to the quantity of lime, iron or bitumen it contains.

The moulds for terra cotta are usu-

GREEK TERRA-COTTA. SELENE & PAN.

ally piece-moulds, made of plaster of Paris, which absorbs much of the moisture of the clay. Sheet clay about 2 in. thick is used. This is carefully pressed into the mould, and supported by webs of clay of the same thickness. It is essential that the clay be uniform throughout, or the shrinkage would be unequal. It is then placed upon a flue to dry, for from two to six hours, when the clay will have contracted sufficiently to allow the mould to be taken off. It is then dried for a further period, and burnt in a kiln. For fine work, the kiln is "muffled"—the "muffle" being a lining of bricks to keep the clay from actual contact with fire and smoke. The dry or semi-dry process is the pressing of clay-powder into metal moulds, which obviates the excessive shrinkage of the wet process. Encaustic tiles are made in this way, the ornament being run into the incised pattern with " slip." Many tiles are decorated in the same way as ordinary earthenware, that is, painted and glazed.

Terra cotta was largely used by the nations of antiquity, especially

GREEK TERRA-COTTA

by the Assyrians, whose clay tablets or books throw so much light upon Assyrian history. With the Greeks, terra cotta was extensively used for antefixæ, and the many beautiful Tanagra figures now treasured in our museums show the exquisite modelling by the Greeks in this material.

This material was used by the Etruscans for their sarcophagi and recumbent figures. The Pompeians tiled their roofs with terra cotta. It was used for votive statues and offerings, and for lamps, some of which were dipped in molten glass.

During the revival of art in Italy in the 15th and 16th centuries, terra cotta was extensively used by the Della Robbia family. Lucca della Robbia produced many beautiful terra cotta reliefs, coated with the white tin enamel and enriched with coloured enamels. Among his numerous works was the marble " Cantoria " or Singing Gallery (1431-40), with its ten panels of sing-ing and dancing figures in relief, which was placed by the organ of S. Maria del Fiore, or Cathedral of Flor-ence. Lucca also executed five marble reliefs, in 1437, for the Campanile, from designs by Giotto, and the two kneeling angels holding can-delabra, in the Sac-risty of the Cathed-ral, Florence, are the only figures in the round by this master.

Among his many beautiful examples

A BAMBINO BY LUCCA S. ANDREA DELLA ROBBIA

of terra cotta are the " Resurrection " and the " Ascension," over the doors of the Sacristy in the Cathedral ; the splendid monument to Bishop Federighi, with its beautiful recumbent figure of marble, in the Church of S. Trinita, Florence ; the Tabernacle of Peretola ; the Madonna of Or San Michele, and the many fine heraldic medallions, with the arms or emblems of the various Guilds, that enrich this beautiful Oratory of Florence (see page 61).

Other heraldic medallions in Florence are the Pazzi and Serristori arms for the Quaratesi Palace, and in the Victoria and Albert Museum are some fine medallions with the arms of King Renè d'Anjou, and twelve medallions representing the months. Most of these examples have the typical quattrocento borders of fruit, flowers, and foliage or fir-cones (fig. 8, plate 27), and are enamelled in brilliant colours.

Ottaviano and Agostino Duccio, contemporary sculptors of repute also collaborated with Lucca in the production of this ware. Andrea della Robbia, the nephew of

TERRA COTTA RELIEF BY ANDREA DELLA ROBBIA.

Lucca, carried on the traditions with rare selective power and artistic skill. Among his early works are the medallions with the *bambini*, for the Loggia of the Spedale degli Innocenti, or Foundling Hospital, at Florence, in collaboration with his uncle, Lucca, and Brunelleschi, the architect. The Adoration and the Annunciation were familiar subjects with Andrea. There is a splendid " Adoration " in the Victoria and Albert Museum.

STIBIUM CASE. ALABASTRON. GREEK OR PHŒNICIAN. WITH A SPIRAL AMPHORA
EGYPTIAN. BRITISH MUSEUM. THREAD IN BLUE.

AMPHORA. VASE.

ROMAN TABLET IN RELIEF THE PORTLAND VASE. ARABIAN ENAMELLED.
WHITE CAMEO ON BLUE GROUND BODY OF DARK BLUE GLASS. LAMP. S.K.M.
MADE IN A MOULD. S.K.M. THE FIGURES IN WHITE.
BRITISH MUSEUM.

VENETIAN ENAMELLED
16TH CENTURY GLASS.

SOUTH KENSINGTON MUSEUM.

VITRO DI TRINA, OR RETICULATED GLASS. VENETIAN BRITISH MUSEUM. SPANISH CUP. GERMAN.
ENAMELLED CUP.

LASS.

The purity of glass, its adaptability to colour, and its remarkable ductility while hot for blowing, twisting, or drawing into threads, differentiates it from all other materials and methods of treatment. Its tradition dates from the remote past, for glass-blowing is represented on the tombs at Thebes (2500 B.C.). It was also used in Egypt for vitreous pastes for bronze and gold cloisonné jewellery, and for the small bottles or Stibium, with chevron patterns, in yellow, turquoise, and white on a coloured ground. Similar patterns, colours, and forms were used by Phœnicia and her colonies. Many remains of bowls were found in Assyria, one of transparent green glass having the name of Sargon (722 B.C.). Greece seems to have imported most of her glass from Phœnicia, but the Romans carried on the tradition, producing fine MOSAIC or MILLEFIORI. This was made by fusing rods of white and coloured glass together, then drawing it out to fine threads, and slicing it transversely ; the section is then placed in a mould and a bubble blown, uniting the mosaic, which is then blown into various shapes. The Romans also used the interlacing of white and coloured rods, called LATICINIO, but they excelled in the CAMEO GLASS, of which the Portland vase is the finest known example. This vase is of dark blue glass, covered with white opaque glass, which was ground away with the wheel, leaving the figures in delicate relief. It was found in 1644 in the sarcophagus of Alexander Severus (A.D. 235), the subject of its relief being the myth of Peleus and Thetis. Another Roman example of cameo glass in the British Museum is the Auldjo vase or Oinochoé, with beautiful reliefs of vine leaves. Frequently these reliefs were blown or pressed into moulds (fig. 6). The tradition then declined until the 14th century, when the Venetians in the Island of Murano perfected the art of glass-making.

The earliest examples of VENETIAN GLASS were massive, richly-gilt, and enamelled in colours. One fine example in the British Museum is signed by its maker, " Magister Aldrevandini." In the 15th and 16th centuries, the most delicate and beautiful blown glass was made, often uncoloured, and with enrichments of knots and wings in blown and shaped blue glass. The Venetians used with equal skill all the old methods of glass-making—the MILLEFIORI ; the LATICINIO, or threads of opaque white enclosing pattern ; RETICELLI, a network of white lines enclosing at the intersections a bubble of air ; and the beautiful VITRO DI TRINA, filigree or lace glass, formed by canes or threads of white or coloured glass being placed in a mould, a bubble being then blown in, and the glass afterwards taken from the mould and blown or twisted to the shape required. The artistic bronze mirrors of ancient and mediæval times now give way to the glass mirrors of the Venetians (A.D. 1500).

EARLY GRISAILLE GLASS. SALISBURY CATHEDRAL

EARLY GOTHIC BORDER FROM BOURGES CATHEDRAL

HERALDIC GLASS FROM OCKWELLS HOUSE. BERKS. 1422-6.

DECORATED GLASS FROM ST MARY'S TRURO.

13TH Century MEDALLION GLASS. SAINT CHAPELLE. PARIS.

STAINED GLASS,

With its depth and translucency, owes its intrinsic qualities to metallic oxides, such as cobalt, giving fine blues, silver, pale and deep yellows, pink from iron and antimony, and ruby from gold and copper, which also yields fine greens. When these oxides are mixed with the glass in its fused state, it is termed "pot-metal," but if the coloured oxides are applied to the surface of the glass only, it is termed "flashed" or "cased glass." Ruby, owing to its depth of colour, is usually cased glass. Fine blues are often flashed, and splendid effects are produced by flashing ruby over yellow or blue pot-metal glass. Cased glass is of the greatest value, owing to the variety of tint that can be produced on a single sheet of glass, and also because the colour may be removed by grinding or by the use of fluoric acid.

The rationale of the glass painter is:—(1) The scheme of composition and colour shown on a small scale; (2) a full-sized cartoon in charcoal or monochrome, with all the details carefully drawn, and showing the lead lines and positions of the iron stanchions for strengthening the window; (3) a tracing on cloth showing the lead lines only, called the cut line, on which are cut the selected pieces of glass; (4) a tracing of the details from the cartoon, with brown enamel, on each piece of glass, the pieces after firing being then fixed in the leading, and kept together with H-shaped leads.

The brown enamel, which is used entirely for outline, detail, or shading, is a fusible glass in combination with opaque manganic or ferric oxide and tar oil. With this enamel, smear shading or stipple shading is worked. This may be removed

PORTION OF A "JESSE" WINDOW, CANTERBURY CATHEDRAL.

as required, before firing, by means of a pointed stick or quill, so as to give the details of embroidery or of heraldic forms.

Silver stain (oxide of silver), introduced at the beginning of the

14th century, is largely used in stained glass, and usually on the back of it. According to the different degrees of heat in the firing, a pale yellow or deep orange of great transparency is produced.

Coloured glass was made by the Egyptians 4,000 years ago, but the earliest stained glass windows recorded were those at Brionde (A.D. 525). None, however, are known to be still in existence prior to those of S. Denis (A.D. 1108). The early examples found in Norman windows have small medallions of figures and ornament of a decided Byzantine type, extremely deep in colour, being, by their style of treatment, termed mosaic glass. The 13th century, or early Gothic period, has single lancet lights, with medallions containing small figures surrounded by the typical 13th century foliage; or the windows were entirely of ornament in *grisaille*, arranged symmetrically—or with a flowing treatment of the vine growing from the recumbent figure of Jesse, and called the " Tree of Jesse "—with narrow bands of ruby or blue, and wide borders. These *grisaille* windows are of a greenish-white glass, with the ornament in outline, and the ground hatched with brown enamel in fine cross lines (figs. 1 and 2). The north transept window at York Cathedral, called the " Five Sisters," is typical of this *grisaille* glass. The finest examples, however, are at Salisbury, Canterbury, and Chartres Cathedrals. Later in the period, single figures were introduced under a simple canopy or gable, plain or crocketed, with an ordinary trefoil arch.

" Quarry " glass, square or diamond in shape, with brown enamel details, was frequently used where simple masses were desired.

In the 14th century, the figures were larger and placed under canopies in each light of the mullioned windows; such figures in

14TH CENTURY HERALDIC GLASS

"QUARRIES," ENGLISH EARLY 16TH CENTURY. (V. & A.M.)

rich colours form a bright belt across the window, surmounted by the canopies, cusped and crocketed, and in strong yellow pot metal, or yellow-cased glass. The borders were narrow, with a somewhat natural rendering of the rose, the maple, and the oak.

In the 15th century a further change took place, figures became more numerous, and the canopy or shrine larger, and chiefly in white glass, with the crockets and finials tipped with yellow stain; a good illustration is that given from All Saints' Church, York. The coloured border of the earlier glass is entirely absent, its place being taken by the shaft of the canopy, and the crockets, finials, and ornaments are square in treatment, and based chiefly on the vine leaf.

Fairford Church perhaps contains the finest series of late Gothic glass (A.D. 1500-30). Like the contemporary architecture of the 16th century, stained glass was now influenced by the Renascence. The canopy still survived, but was horizontal or pedimental in form, with purely classical columns and details. Good examples of this period are the windows of King's College Chapel, Cambridge (1520), where rich Renascence work is introduced into late Gothic mullioned windows. These windows are probably similar to those by Barnard Flower, glazier, placed in Henry the Seventh's Chapel at Westminster Abbey, as in Henry the Seventh's will it was expressly provided that " the walles, doores, windows, archies, and vaults and ymagies of the same, of our said chapell, within and without be painted, garnisshed, and adorned with our armes, bagies, cognoisaunts, and other convenient painteng, in so goodly and riche manner as suche a werk requireth, and to a King's werk apperteigneth ' :—" that the windows of our said chapell be glased with stores [? stories]. ymagies, armes, bagies, and cognoisaunts."

Of this glass little remains, but we know that a contract was made in the time of Henry the Eighth to complete the windows of King's College Chapel, Cambridge, " with good, clene, sure, and perfyte glasse, and oryent colors and imagery of the story of the old lawe and of the new lawe, after the forme, maner, goodenes, curiousytie, and clenelynes, in every poynt of the glasse windowes of the Kynge's new Chapell at Westminster." This glass was by Francis Williamson and Simon Symonds, glaziers, of London, and its cost was to be sixteen pence per foot. Galyen

LATE GOTHIC WINDOW, NORTH AISLE, ALL SAINTS' CHURCH, YORK.

Hoon, Richard Bownde, Thomas Reve, and James Nicholson also agreed to execute eighteen windows of the upper storey of King's College Chapel, similar to those at Westminster by Barnard Flower, six of the windows to be set up within twelve months, and the bands of leads to be at the rate of twopence per foot.

At Warwick, the windows of the Beauchamp Chapel were glazed by John Pruddle, of Westminster, " with the best, cleanest, and strongest glasse of beyond the sea that may be had in England, and of the finest colours of blew, yellow, red, purpure, sanguine, and violet, and all other colours that shall be most necessary and best to make and embellish the matters, images, and stories that shall be delivered and appointed by the said executors by patterns in paper, afterwards to be traced and pictured by another painter, in rich colours, at the charges of the said glazier."

About 1540, transparent enamels were introduced with skill and reticence, but gradually glass painters began to vie with pictorial oil painting in effects of light and shade, the ground work or material losing that beautiful translucent or transmitted colour which is the chief glory of stained glass. An example showing the degradation of this art is the west window of New College, Oxford, painted by Jervas, in 1777, from designs by Sir Joshua Reynolds.

In the 14th century, the English craftsman attained a thorough mastery over his materials, and consequently the type of ornament followed English contemporary architecture more closely.

To sum up, stained glass changed through the different periods from the rich coloured mosaic of the Normans, the equally rich coloured medallions and *grisaille* glass of the early Gothic, the decorated Gothic, with glass in lighter colours and a prevalence of yellow stain, culminating in the later Gothic period, when largeness of mass, lightness, and silvery colour were the characteristics.

ST. ELIZABETH OF HUN-
GARY, GERMAN, 15TH
CENT.

A beautiful treatment of stained glass, dating from the 15th century, was used by the Arabians. This glass, which has a singular gem-like quality, and is without enamel or stain, was let into a framework of plaster, which had been cut and pierced with geometrical or floral patterns.

ENAMELS.

Of the many decorative arts, enamelling is one of the most beautiful, having a singular charm of limpid or opalescent colour of great purity, richness, and durability, and being capable of a most refined and varied treatment for the enrichment of metals.

Enamel is a vitreous or glass compound, translucent or opaque, owing its colouring properties to mineral oxides, or sulphides, a fine opaque white being produced by oxide of tin. These enamels require different degrees of heat in order to fuse them and to cause their adhesion to the metal. Enamels are divided into three classes :—CLOISONNÉ, CHAMPLEVÉ, and PAINTED ENAMELS.

CLOISONNÉ enamel is that in which the cloisons or cells are formed by soldering thin, flat wire of metal upon a plate of copper, the cloisons being filled with the various enamels, in powder or in paste ; then, in order to vitrify the enamel, it is heated in a kiln, if upon a flat surface, or by the aid of a blow-pipe if upon a curved surface.

Cloisonné was in use from the early dynasties in Egypt, many fine large pectorals having been found in the tombs. These usually have the form of a hawk and are of gold or bronze with well-defined cloisons, which were filled with carefully fitted coloured paste or glass, and this undoubtedly was the origin of the true or vitreous cloisonné enamel. Byzantine enamel is invariably cloisonné, and one of the most beautiful examples of this period is the Pala d'Oro of S. Mark's at Venice (A.D. 976, see page 135). Perhaps the Chinese and Japanese have carried this cloisonné to its greatest perfection in softness of colour and beauty of technique. The earliest Chinese cloisonné such as that deposited at Nara is of the 8th century; after a considerable lapse of time it reappears in the 13th and 14th centuries.

Early Japanese cloisonné was doubtless derived from Chinese sources, and it is characterized by extremely thin beaten copper grounds and the frequent use of a dark green ground in place of the dark blue of the Chinese cloisonné.

The Japanese cloisonné reached its culmination during the last century, when many splendid examples of refined and delicate enamels were produced, remarkable for their beautiful opalescent and translucent colour. Gold cloisons with opaque and translucent enamels were frequently inserted in iron or silver objects by the Japanese of this period.

An early example of English cloisonné is the jewel of King Alfred (page 133). A fine Celtic cloisonné treatment may be seen in the Ardagh chalice (page 133), where the cloisons were cut out of a plate of silver and embedded in the enamel while soft. The Celtic craftsmen also had a beautiful treatment of enamelling by engraving or pressing a pattern in intaglio or sunk relief, on an enamelled ground, and then filling these intaglios with other enamels.

A most exquisite kind of enamel called " *Plique à Jour* " was used by the Byzantines : this was composed of open filigree cloisons, filled with translucent enamels.

CHAMPLEVÉ enamel is formed by engraving, casting or scooping out the cloisons from a metal plate, leaving a thin wall or boundary between each cloison, which is then filled with the various enamels as in the cloisonné method. This Champlevé method was practised in Britain before the Roman Conquest, and was probably derived from the Phœnicians, who, centuries before the Romans came to England, had traded with Cornwall for tin. The beauty of colour and perfect adaptability of these early enamelled brooches, fibulæ and trappings of horses of the early Britons and Celts, are remarkable, showing a fine sense of colour and a harmony of line and mass. A splendid bronze Celtic shield (fig. 6, plate 17), now in the British Museum, is enriched with fine bosses of red enamel. These Champlevé enamels upon bronze have usually an opalescent or cloudy appearance caused by the fusion of the tin in the bronze alloy during firing. Champlevé enamels were used with rare skill and refinement to enhance the beautiful art of the goldsmith during the Middle Ages ; the Chalice, the Paten, the Reliquary, the Thurible, the Crozier, and the bookcovers of the Churches, especially, were enriched with beautiful enamels. Classed among the Champlevé enamels is that method called JEWELLER'S ENAMEL or "*Baisse Taille*," in which the plate is engraved in low relief or beaten up in repoussé and then flooded with translucent enamel. The Lynn cup of the time of Richard II. is one of the oldest pieces of corporation plate and is covered with fine translucent blue and green enamels (plate 60).

In India, where fine colour is a splendid tradition, Champlevé enamel soon attained a remarkable perfection of technique and purity and brilliance of colour almost unknown to the Western nations. The Champlevé enamels of JAIPUR have most beautiful lustrous and transparent blues, greens, and reds laid on a pure gold ground. PERTUBGHUR is renowned for the fine green or turquoise enamel fired upon a plate of gold ; while the enamel was still soft a plate of pierced gold was pressed into the enamel. This pierced plate was afterwards engraved with incidents of history or hunting. In RATAIN, in Central India, a similar enamel is made having a fine blue in place of the Pertubghur green.

The fine monumental brasses, of which many still remain in our English cathedrals and churches, are a survival of the Champlevé process, the cloisons being usually filled with a black NIELLO, but occasionally the heraldic shields are enriched with coloured enamels. During the 11th and 12th centuries, LIMOGES was renowned for its Champlevé enamels, but early in the 15th century PAINTED ENAMELS were introduced, and Limoges became the centre of this art, called late Limoges or GRISAILLE ENAMEL.

The enamel colours were now used as a pigment, and were painted and fired upon a copper plate. The enrichments in grisaille, or grey and white were used upon a black, violet or dark blue ground, the grisaille afterwards being enriched with details of fine gold lines. These Limoges enamels have a splendid technique, but they lack the charms of the luminous colour and judicious use of enamels of the early Champlevé period. The most renowned masters of the painted enamels of Limoges were the Penicaud family, Courtois, Pierre Raymond, and Leonard Limousin. About 1600-1650 Jean Toutin and his pupil Petitot produced some fine

LIMOGES ENAMELLED DISH BY PIERRE RAYMOND.

painted miniatures in opaque enamels upon gold, remarkable for delicacy and perfection of enamelling. About 1750 painted enamel was introduced into England, and produced at Battersea later, and in Bilston and Wednesbury in South Staffordshire. The enrichment consisted of ornaments painted in natural colours on a white ground.

BATTERSEA ENAMEL

The finest enamels undoubtedly are those in which the enamel is used in small quantities, such as in the Celtic jewellery, the bookcovers, and the Church and Corporation plate of the Gothic and early Renascence period, and the early Byzantine cloisonné, such as the Hamilton brooch in the British Museum, and the Pala d'Oro of S. Mark's, Venice, which was made at Constantinople for the Doge Orseolo in A.D. 976, and has 83 panels of fine cloisonné enamel set in a framework of gold.

The " *Plique à jour*," the " *Baisse taille* " and the Pertubghur enamels are fine examples of appropriateness of treatment with translucency or opalescence and richness of colour.

The Japanese cloisonné with its literal treatment of natural forms, and the painted enamel portraits of Francis I. and contemporary princes by Leonard Limousin, clever as they undoubtedly are, lack the depth and purity of colour obtained by the early methods. Frequently, however, the Penicauds, Nardou and Jean I., and II., obtained some richness in the painted enamels by the use of " *Paillons* " or pieces of metallic foil which were afterwards flooded with translucent enamel. Although pictorial rather than purely ornamental in treatment, the work of Henry Bone (1755-1834) deserves mention here, as an English achievement unique of its kind.

ROMAN
SILVER CUPS.
FROM THE TREASURE-TROVE
OF HILDESHEIM. BERLIN.

OCTAGONAL
GOLD VESSEL. PART
OF THE TREASURE OF PETROSSA
BUKAREST MUSEUM.

THE TARA
BROOCH.
10TH CENTURY
DUBLIN

THE
LIMERICK
CROSIER.
SILVER GILT
PASTORAL
STAFF,
ENRICHED WITH
TRANSLUCENT
ENAMELS.
IRISH.
EARLY
15TH CENTURY.

THE LYNN CUP
SILVER GILT
& ENAMELLED
ENGLISH
14TH CENTURY
CORPORATION OF
KINGS LYNN.

DESIGN FOR
QUEEN JANE
SEYMOUR'S
GOLD CUP
BY HOLBEIN
1536
BODLEIAN
LIBRARY,
OXFORD

OLD AND SILVER.

With their intrinsic value, ductility, and beauty of colour, Gold and Silver have long been associated with the decorative arts of the past, and the many splendid examples still in existence are a tribute to the culture and personality of the craftsman.

Beautiful early examples were found in 1859 with the mummy of Queen Aah-Hotep (1800 B.C., Cairo Museum), and consisted of bracelets, armlets, rings, chains, a diadem, a small model of a war galley, and a poniard, all of exquisite workmanship and of pure gold, enriched with jasper and turquoise vitreous pastes. At Petrossa, in 1837 (Bukharest Museum), some splendid gold objects of Byzantine workmanship were found, consisting of two neck-rings or Torques, a large salver, hammered and chased, a ewer, a bowl with figures in repoussé, four fibulæ enriched with precious stones, a gorget, and two double-handled cups (plate 60). At Guarrazar, in Spain, ten gold votive crowns of Gothic workmanship were found : one inscribed with the name of King Suintila (A.D. 630) is now in the Museum at Madrid ; the others are in the Hotel Cluny, Paris, the largest having the name of King Rescesvinthus (A.D. 670) in pendive letters.

Of silversmiths' work, the most important is the " Treasure of Hildesheim," found in 1868 (Berlin Museum), consisting of thirty objects, cups, vases, and dishes, beautiful in contour and admirably enriched with delicate repoussé work of the Greco-Roman period (plate 60).

Of the gold and silver vessels used by Solomon in the temple, we have only a representation of the seven-branched golden candlestick on the Arch of Titus, at Rome.

GOLDEN CANDLESTICK FROM THE ARCH OF TITUS, ROME.

THE ARDAGH CHALICE. CELTIC, X" Century.

English work of an early date is rare, but there are two very beautiful examples, one, the gold ring of Ethelwulf, enriched with blue Champlevé enamel, now in the British Museum, and Alfred's jewel of gold, with cloisonné, opaque, and translucent enamels, with the inscription : " Alfred me has worked " : this is, with the single exception of the S. Ambrose altar-frontal, the oldest signed enamel extant (871-901, Ashmolean Museum, Oxford).

Contemporary Irish work was even more skilful, and the Ardagh chalice of silver, with gold filigree and enamel enrichments, and the Tara brooch (plate 60) are fine examples.

133

ENGLISH
SILVER·WORK

1

2

3

4

GRACE·CUP.
SILVER·GILT
&·ENAMELLED
MERCERS
COMPANY.
1500.

SALT·CELLAR
SILVER·GILT
NEW·COLLEGE
OXFORD
1490

SILVER·GILT
SALT·CELLAR
CORPUS
CHRISTI
COLLEGE.
CAM-
BRIDGE
1560

SILVER·GILT
STANDING
CUP.
St·JOHN'S
COLLEGE.
CAMBRIDGE·
1615-6

5

6

CHALICE

7

PIX
A·VESSEL
TO·CONTAIN
THE·CON-
SECRATED
WAFER.

8

THURIBLE
OR·INCENSE
BURNER
14th·Cent

CORPUS·CHRISTI·COLLEGE·1507.
CAMBRIDGE.

S·K·M
15th·Century

14th·Century
St·MARKS
VENICE

CLUNY
MUSEUM

9

SILVER
BOWL
1685
AT·KNOLE

10

11

SILVER
VASE·BY
R·ADAM
1770

S·K·M

GOLD
CUP.
EXETER
COLLEGE.
OXFORD.
1660-70.

12

13

SILVER
CANDELABRUM
S·K·M.
1714.

14

SILVER
PUNCH-
BOWL
VINTNERS
HALL·
1702

15

SILVER
VASE.
1770.

S·K·M

THE
RICH·CUP
SADDLERS
HALL·1681.

The wealth and elaborate ritual of the mediæval church called forth the finest effort of the craftsman, more especially the gold and silversmiths, who in England, perhaps more than in other countries, produced abundant examples of ecclesiastical plate. Altar-frontals of gold, used only on rare festivals, are some of the richest relics of the past. An early example (11th century) was given by the Emperor Henry II. to the Cathedral of Basle (Cluny Museum). It is of gold, 3 ft. high and 5 ft. 6 in. wide, and has many figures in relief. At S. Ambrose, Milan, is an altar-frontal of silver-gilt, set with precious stones and enamels, and signed by " Wolvinus," an Anglo-Saxon, and dated A.D. 838. The great altar-frontal or Pala d'Oro of S. Mark's, Venice, was commenced in 976 at Constantinople. It is 9 ft. 9 in. wide and 6 ft. 6 in. high, consisting of 83 plaques of gold, on which are figures of our Saviour, angels, and saints in cloisonné enamels, and set with precious stones.

The early two-handled chalices were frequently very large, and it is recorded that Charlemagne gave one of pure gold, set with precious stones, and weighing 53 lbs., to S. Peter's at Rome. From the 12th century the chalice became smaller and without handles, and the bowl semi-ovid or conical. The knob or boss on the stem, together with the base, are usually lobed or hexafoil, and enriched with repoussé work and enamels (plate 61).

The pax, introduced in the 13th century, was a small rectangular plaque, used in the celebration of the Mass to convey the kiss of peace. The cross, the shrine, the reliquary, the pix, the ciborium, the monstrance, the thurible or censer were of gold and silver, enriched with jewels and enamels or delicate repoussé work.

The pastoral staff, or crosier, was first a staff of wood, capped by a ball or knob with a simple volute ; then later the knob developed into tabernacle work, with canopies and figures, and the volute or crook, enriched with crockets, frequently enclosed the *Agnus Dei* (Lamb of God) or other sacred group. The early crosiers (12th or 13th centuries) were usually of copper, gilt and enamelled, and of Limoges workmanship. From the 14th century, gold, silver, and ivory were the materials generally used. The Limerick crosier is a good illustration of this period (plate 60).

Contemporary with this splendid ecclesiastical work was the college and corporation plate, of which the Lynn Cup (plate 60) is perhaps one of the most beautiful among many magnificent examples extant. The Leigh Cup (plate 61, fig. 1) and salt-cellar (fig. 2) are also of the Gothic period, but with the first half of the 16th century the Renascence appears in the works of the great goldsmiths, such as Benvenuto Cellini, of Italy ; Etienne de Laune, of France ; and Jamnitzer, of Germany. With Holbein's design for a gold cup (plate 60) the English Renascence appears, and civic plate was enriched with strap-work and cartouches, with foliated pendants of fruit and flowers (figs. 3 and 4, plate 61). In the 17th century, the acanthus foliage, with delicate chasing and relief, is the chief feature.

1 PORTION OF GRILLE. 13TH CENTURY. WINCHESTER CATHEDRAL.

2 EARLY NORMAN HINGE. HARTLEY CHURCH, KENT.

3 EARLY NORMAN HINGE. SEMPERINGHAM CHURCH, LINCOLNSHIRE.

4 EARLY ENGLISH HINGE. WESTMINSTER ABBEY.

5 DIAGRAM OF ONE OF THE HINGES, NOTRE DAME, PARIS.

6 ONE OF THE SCROLLS OF THE NOTRE DAME HINGES. 13TH CENTURY.

7 ENTRANCE GRILLE, WYNYARD PARK. DATE 1648.

8 GRILLE, ST PAULS CATHEDRAL.

9 WINDOW GRILLE, BRESCIA. BEATEN WORK & SHIELDS, BOLTED TO THE BARS.

10 BALCONY GRILLE AT VERSAILLES. LOUIS XIV.

11 WROUGHT IRON CORNUCOPIA. MUSEUM FLORENCE.

12 KEYS FROM THE SPITZER COLLECTION. 17TH Century GERMAN. 16TH Century FRENCH.

13 PORTION OF ENTRANCE GRILLE FROM HAMPTON COURT BY THE FRENCH SMITH, TIJOU, 1695. NOW IN SOUTH KENSINGTON MUSEUM.

14 15th Century LOCK, CLUNY MUSEUM.

15 13TH Century GRILLE, SANTA CROCE, FLORENCE.

(3) MIDDLE OF GATES, S. PAUL'S CATHEDRAL. BY JEAN TIJOU.

(2) GATES AT ST. MARY'S, REDCLIFFE, BRISTOL. BY WILLIAM EDNEY, 1710.

(1) "OVERTHROW" OR CRESTING OF GATES, S. PAUL'S CATHEDRAL. BY JEAN TIJOU.

ROUGHT IRON-WORK.

The decorative qualities of iron, with its strength, durability, and comparative cheapness, have rendered it one of the most useful metals in the applied arts. Many fine Norman hinges of wrought iron are still in existence, having a straight central bar or strap, with small scroll terminations; these central straps were strengthened with crescent-shaped pieces, terminating in small serpent forms, probably a survival of the Viking traditions. This form of hinge was succeeded by the early Gothic hinge, which was a series of spirals springing from the straight bar or strap, the spiral being welded or fastened with collars; these spirals were enriched with a three-lobbed foliage, or trefoil, typical of the early Gothic period; fine examples of this hinge occur on the west door of Notre Dame, Paris, where this typical spiral has the trefoil leaf, with birds, dragons, and small rosettes in stamped iron. This stamped characteristic may be seen, but in a less degree, in the fine hinges of Leighton Buzzard Church, Eaton Bray Church, Bedfordshire, and the Eleanor grill in Westminster Abbey, by Thomas de Leghton, in 1294. In the 14th and 15th centuries, when panelled doors took the place of the earlier doors, this early Gothic style of hinge was not needed (fig. 5), so that we find no trace of it in that period, but the art of wrought iron was continued with the hammered and chiselled hinges and lock plates of the most varied and delicate workmanship, which enriched the beautiful Gothic chests of the 14th and 15th centuries. The simple wrought screen, which was so largely used in the 13th century, was now elaborated, especially in Italy, and fine examples of quatre-foil grilles with massive wrought framing and a rich frieze of foliage, cupids, and animals in pierced and hammered iron are to be seen at the cathedrals of Orvieto, Prato, and Siena, dating from about 1337 to 1350, and at Santa Croce, Florence (1371); but it was in Spain and France that the screen reached its culmination. The Spanish screens or " Réjas " in the cathedrals of Seville, Toledo, and Granada have a fine range of turned and chiselled vertical bars, some 30 to 50 ft high, with an elaborate frieze and cresting.

The wrought iron gate piers in St. George's Chapel, Windsor, with their architectural treatment of open panelling, cresting, and massive buttresses, are filed, bolted, and riveted, and are splendid examples of Flemish workmanship, probably by Quentin Matsys.

In England, after a period of decided eclipse during the 17th century, many fine examples of wrought iron gates and grilles were produced during the early part of the 18th century; Jean Tijou, whose chief works are at Hampton Court and S. Paul's Cathedral (1690-1710), (plate 63, figs. 1 and 3), was followed by Robert Bateman, of Derby, the brothers Roberts, of North Wales, William Edney, of Bristol (plate 63, fig. 2), and the London Smiths, Robinson, Warren, and Buncker, whose skilful and artistic work, produced from 1707-20, is still extant in many parts of the country.

1 ASSYRIAN BRONZE BRACELET. LOUVRE.

2 INCISED DESIGN ON ETRUSCAN MIRROR. ATHENA, HERMES & PERSEUS. BRITISH MUSEUM.

3 BRONZE TRIPOD FROM POMPEI.

4 ONE OF THE BRONZES OF SIRIS 6¾" IN HEIGHT PORTION OF GREEK ARMOUR. BRONZE REPOUSSÉ. BRITISH MUSEUM.

5 LAMP OR CANDLESTICK. ITALIAN, 1570. SOUTH KENSINGTON MUSEUM.

6 KNOCKER FORMED OF DOLPHINS & SATYRS. ITALIAN. 1570. S.K. MUSEUM.

7 BRONZE LAMP FROM HERCULANEUM IN THE MUSEUM AT NAPLES.

8 CANDELABRA FROM HERCULANEUM NAPLES MUSEUM.

9 BRONZE KNOCKER. FROM THE PALAZZO TREVISAN VENICE. 16TH CENTURY.

10 SUSPENDED LAMP IN PISA CATHEDRAL BY TACCA. 1600.

11 CANDELABRA FROM HERCULANEUM, 79 A.D. IN THE MUSEUM AT NAPLES.

12 BRONZE GRILLE IN THE CATHEDRAL, PRATO, FROM A DESIGN BY BRUNELLESCHI.

BRONZES.

Bronze, an alloy of copper and tin, has been in use from a remote period ; its adaptability for casting, its durability and colour, to say nothing of the fine green patûre, render this material one of extreme beauty and usefulness. Among the many examples of antiquity are the 1,000 statues of Osiris, found in the temple of Rameses III., and the bands of figure subjects in relief from the Assyrian Balawat gates, now in the British Museum. In Greece, bronze was wrought with exquisite skill and refinement, and the name of Lysippos (340 B.C.) is usually associated with the finest statues.

Two beautiful repoussé bronzes (fig. 4) probably by Lysippos, found in 1820 near the river Siris, in Italy, are admirable examples of this period. Many Greek statues have been found in Pompeii and Herculaneum, of which the beautiful statuette of Narcissus is the best known, and many bronze heads are still extant with the eyes formed of ivory or beautiful stones and jewels.

Etruscan bronzes have a most expressive treatment of incised lines, which differentiates them from the repoussé work of the Greeks The bronze mirrors with an incised treatment of classic mythology (fig. 2), and the cistæ, or toilet caskets, all found, with but few exceptions, at Palestrina, are typical of Etruscan bronzes. Of small decorative bronzes, Naples Museum alone has over 14,000 examples, consisting of candelabra, tripods (figs. 3, 7, 8, and 11), tables, chairs, and couches, which eighteen centuries ago were used by wealthy Roman citizens. The well-known winged " Victory " of Brescia is a beautiful example, reminiscent of a Greek statue.

Early bronze equestrian statues are the " Nero " found at Pompeii (Naples Museum), and the " Marcus Aurelius " at Rome (A.D. 175, plate 65). The four bronze horses, now in front of S. Mark's, at Venice, are probably of the time of Nero. Many fine mediæval English bronze effigies are still extant, replacing earlier effigies of Purbeck marble, such as the Earl of Salisbury at Salisbury (1227), and the earliest recumbent figures in gilded bronze are those of Henry III. (1272), and Queen Eleanor (1291), in Westminster Abbey, by William Torell, goldsmith of London. In Canterbury Cathedral is the fine effigy of the Black Prince (1376). The Richard II. and his Queen, in Westminster Abbey, are by Nicholas Broker and Geoffrey Prest (1395), and at Warwick is the magnificent Earl of Warwick, by William Austin and Thomas Stevens (1453). Later examples are the " Gattamelata " at Padua, by Donatello (1453), the magnificent " Colleone " at Venice (plate 65), by Verrochio and Leopardi, and the " Louis XIV." by Girardon, cast by Jean Baltazar Keller in 1699, and destroyed in the French Revolution.

The Florentine Torregiano in 1512, made the beautiful recumbent effigies of Henry VII. and his Queen (see page 81), and also the Countess of Richmond, which are in Westminster Abbey, where there are also the gilded bronzes of the Duke of Buckingham (1628), and the

EQUESTRIAN STATUE OF BARTOLOMEO COLEONE. BY ANDREA VERROCCHIO & ALESSANDRO LEOPARDO. A.D.1488. VENICE.

EQUESTRIAN STATUE OF MARCUS AURELIUS. ROME. A.D.175.

1554.

ONE GATE OF BAPTISTERY AT FLORENCE, BY LORENZO GHIBERTI.

STATUE OF PERSEUS BY CELLINI. FLORENCE.

Duke and Duchess of Richmond (1623), by an unknown artist. The statue of Charles I. by Le Sueur, and the Charles II. at Chelsea, and the James II. at Whitehall, by Grinling Gibbons, are later English examples of bronzes.

In Rome, the recumbent effigies of Sixtus IV. (1493), and Innocent VIII., which are the finest of Renascence bronzes, were by Antonio Pollajuolo. In 1508 Michel Angelo made the colossal seated statue of Pope Julius II., which was over the door of S. Petronio at Bologna. Benvenuto Cellini was the great Florentine goldsmith; his " Nymph of Fontainebleau," a relief in bronze for the lunette over the door of the Palace, is now in the Louvre, but his masterpiece is the " Perseus " (plate 65), in the Loggia dei Lanzi, at Florence, where the " Judith and Holofernes " by Donatello is also placed. Another eminent master was Giovanni da Bologna, who executed the beautiful fountain with the figure of Neptune, at Bologna.

The Shrine of S. Sebald at Nuremberg, by Peter Vischer (1508-9), and the figure of the Emperor Maximilian at Innsbruck, by Lodovico Scalza, of Milan, which is enclosed by an elaborate grille, and surrounded by twenty-eight large bronze statues of men in armour, are excellent examples of German Renascence.

GILT BRONZE MADE IN 1786 BY BOIZOT FOR
MARIE ANTOINETTE; MOUNTS BY THOMIRE.

Many of the early historical buildings still retain their original bronze gates. Those of the Pantheon (A.D. 118-38), are still in position, also those of the cathedral at Hildesheim, with the panels of scriptural subjects in high relief, and the name and date of Bishop Bernward (1015). Early Byzantine gates cast at Constantinople by Staurachios, are at Amalfi (1066), and at S. Salvator, Atrani (1087), enriched with figures in silver damascening.

The west door of San Zeno, Verona (12th century), is of wood, covered with panels of repoussé work. Early cast bronze gates in Italy are those of S. Ambrogio, Milan (1170), and at Trani, Ravello, and Monreale Cathedral (by Bonanno, 1186), having relief panels and bosses upon the styles of the door. In 1150, Bonanno cast some gates for the cathedral at Pisa, which were destroyed, with the exception of one, by fire in 1596, the west door being replaced in 1600 by a fine work by Giovanni da Bologna.

The noble gates to Henry VII.'s Chapel at Westminster, dating from the commencement of the 16th century, are of bronze. With their fine panels and well-executed heraldic devices and animals they represent the highest type of Gothic design.

141

PIERCED, CHASED, & ENGRAVED METAL-WORK.

Apart from screens, balconies, door-mounts, and the like, there were—more especially from *c.* A.D. 1500— endless varieties of applied metal-work, of which our limits only permit a casual mention.

Down to the 16th century, armour, whether for the field or the lists, had been, on the whole, sparing of ornamentation. Weapons, too, other than mere "processional" pieces, never sacrificed practical considerations to display. But after 1500 a more florid style of decoration intrudes itself increasingly, even into military and tournament equipment; engraving, etching, embossing, and inlays of gold and silver. Highly ornate work of this kind is associated with the greatest armourers of the age, such as the Negroli brothers, and Lucio Piccinino of Milan, or the Colman family, and Anton Peffenhauser of Augsburg. Pierced chiselled work also occurs, but mainly restricted to the guards and mounts of sword, dagger, or to ceremonial "hafted weapons" (halberds, partisans, glaves,

ITALIAN 16TH CENTURY RICHLY ORNAMENTED BREASTPLATE.

etc.). Especially beautiful examples are the Italian and Spanish cup-hilted rapiers (with their daggers) of the 17th century, the pierced design resembling fine point lace.

Clasps, hinges, and mounts for various purposes, and outer cases for books also illustrate the engraving, piercing, and chasing of metal. Heraldic motives (*cf.* plate 66 (2)) are frequently introduced. Another fruitful field for fine work was provided by locks and keys, while the 17th and 18th century clocks and watches are extensively adorned with fine engraved and saw-cut metal, and metal mounts for furniture provide a fruitful field for study.

WATCH FACE, SILVER AND
ENGRAVED COPPER.
FRENCH, EARLY 17TH CENT.

WATCHCOCK PATTERNS, BY DANIEL MAROT, *circa* 1700.

PIERCED AND HERALDIC ORNAMENT.

Plate 66.

(1) SILVER BOOK-COVER IN CHASED OPENWORK, GERMAN, LATE 17TH OR EARLY 18TH CENTURY.

(2) PIERCED COVER FOR A BIBLE, WITH ARMS OF SAXONY, ETC. WURTEMBERG, 1575.

(3) A STONEWARE MUG, SIEGBURG, PRUSSIA, 1589.

HERALDIC ORNAMENT.

Heraldry was, in its origins, severely practical. As, during the course of the 12th century, the knight grew to be " sheathed in complete steel," it became important for him to bear distinctive and conspicuous marks by which he might be known to friend and foe alike. The earliest traces of Heraldry thus date from the 12th century, though the science was probably not reduced to a regular code till well into the 13th. The knight's colours and armorial bearings were originally displayed upon his shield, surcoat, and horse's trappings, and his crest above his helmet ; but the men of the Middle Ages, quick to perceive the decorative possibilities of their devices, soon applied them to architectural ornament, furniture, books, plate, and even to garments.

Whereas the spirit of heraldry declined with the Middle Ages, its ingenious adaptation to the most varied objects throughout the 16th century, and even later, continually provoke our admiration. Heraldry, applied as an engraved, stamped, cut, or modelled decoration is, as countless examples go to prove, a genuine embellishment in its fit place. The skill with which Dürer has worked heraldic designs into his engraved compositions is especially noteworthy, and his contemporaries, Beham, Burgkmair, Weiditz, and many others, produced a volume of fine work in decorative heraldry.

It should be noticed that, down to the 17th century, when it was not feasible to render appropriate " tinctures " and " metals " by means of paints or enamels, colours were simply ignored. Various systems of hatching and cross-hatching were then introduced to express colour by black and white.

HERALDIC PANELS FROM THE BRASS OF JOHN I., DUKE OF CLEVES, *circa* 1481.

143

BRASS OF JOHN LIMEBORCH, LUBECK, 1474.
FROM AN ORIGINAL RUBBING. SCALE ·8″ = 1 FOOT.

BRASSES AND INCISED SLABS.

A form of art much associated with England is the monumental brass. It appears to derive, on the one hand, from the kindred incised stone slab, on the other from Limoges enamel work. In general treatment it is but an improvement of the former, while from the latter it borrows the occasional introduction of enamel, or some coloured substitute, into the heraldic motives.

Although brasses were at one time in common use in France, Belgium, and Germany, it would appear that England at all times held premier place for the number of such memorials. At the Dissolution of the Monasteries there were in existence about 150,000 such brasses, of which only a fortieth part remains to-day. But though various causes have reduced our heritage, the religious and other wars abroad have wrought far greater havoc.

Though the earlier brasses contain little but the figure of the deceased and an appropriate inscription, from about 1320 we meet with the ornamental canopy, often embellished with heraldic or symbolic motives. The Continental brass in particular, whose background was of *solid* brass,[1] admitted of very lavish decoration. Architectural and heraldic motives and rich diapers cover the whole field, adding immensely to the effect. It may be worth while to remark that whereas in England the earliest brasses (1277-1400) are undoubtedly the finest, a rapid decline being noticeable after 1500, the Continental brasses of the 15th and 16th centuries are often full of technical skill and vigour. Such fine examples as those at Meissen, Lubeck (see plate 67), Bruges, and elsewhere, show a remarkable mastery over the material, and great minuteness of detail. The cross-hatching and shading, however reprehensible in principle, is at least the work of firm and practised hands, and very different to the meaningless scratches that often pass for shading with our own craftsmen.

PORTION OF A BORDER ILLUSTRATING THE AGES OF MAN. BRASS OF
PIETER LANSAME AND WIFE, YPRES, 1487-89.

[1] The English brass was cut out and laid upon a stone matrix.

1 RENASCENCE TABLE. BARDINI COLLECTION LATE 16TH CENTURY

2 BY DV CERCEAU

3 GRÆCO-ROMAN MARBLE TABLE POMPEII.

4 5 TWO LATE RENASCENCE TABLES, CLUNY MUSEUM.

6 CARVED CASSONE, ITALIAN, 16TH CENTURY. SOUTH KENSINGTON MUSEUM

7 CORONATION CHAIR WESTMINSTER ABBEY. EDWARD I

RENASCENCE CHAIRS, CLUNY MUSEUM

8 9 10

DECORATIVE FURNITURE.

Caskets, chests, and cabinets, chairs, tables, couches, and bedsteads have been of universal use during many ages, differentiated in design and craftsmanship according to the culture, wealth, and customs of the people, and the versatility, inventiveness, and skill of the craftsman. Many materials have been used for furniture, the chief being wood of various kinds, which was selected for its constructive qualities, beautiful texture, grain, and colour, and its adaptability to carving and inlay.

The universal use of the chair has doubtless tended to preserve its

EGYPTIAN.
THRONE OF QUEEN HATSHEPSU.
XVIII DYNASTY.
BRITISH MUSEUM.
DARK WOOD WITH GILDING.

EGYPTIAN CHAIR. FROM THE TOMB OF RAMESES III. B.C. 1200.

ASSYRIAN CHAIR.
FROM A BAS-RELIEF

FROM A GREEK VASE 400 B.C.

typical form through many centuries, and though undergoing various modifications, it has still retained its essential character as a seat. Numerous illustrations of early chairs are found on the carved reliefs of ancient Egypt and Assyria, and there are in the British Museum some early Egyptian chairs, one of which is of ebony, with uprights turned in the lathe, and inlaid with ivory. Many Greek chairs, remarkable for their simple and beautiful form, are shown upon the early Greek vases; and the Roman "Sella Curulis," or chair of senators and consuls, is represented on the Byzantine ivories (plate 72, fig. 9).

The Chair of S. Peter, of the 1st century A.D., which has enrichments of ivory and gold, is purely architectonic in form, and the same may be said of the coronation chair (fig. 7), which is the earliest example extant in England. The Gothic chairs, few of which remain, were of the box form, with carved linen-fold panels. During the age of Elizabeth, chairs were of oak, with turned supports, the back having an arcade in low relief or in open work. This form of chair was continued during the reign of James I., when the "Farthingale Chair" was introduced. In the middle years of the 17th century the chairs had twisted supports and rails, the back and seat being covered with hide or with stamped and coloured leather. In

VENETIAN CHAIR.
XVI. CENTURY.

the reign of Charles II. and James II. the twisted or carved and scrolled form of legs were common, with the seat and portion of back in cane, and the back, cresting, and rails in richly-carved open work, similar to fig. 10. In the time of William and Mary, the long supports were turned, and the front supports and arms turned and scrolled, the back of the chair being either of open work, or upholstered and stuffed. The chairs with simple curved or cabriole front legs, the arms, seat, and back upholstered with cut velvets, are characteristic of the early 18th century.

With George II. and III. we come to the use of mahogany and the work of Thomas Chippendale, who published a work on furniture

HEPPLEWHITE. SHERATON.

in 1754. His chairs have frequently straight legs, with shallow sunk carving, or the carved cabriole leg and claw foot; the back is of open work of scrolls, strapwork, or ribbon-work, with delicate carving. Mathias Lock issued a book on furniture in 1765. In 1789, the *Guide*, a set of designs by George Hepplewhite, was published. Much of his work is refined and delicate in treatment and distinctive in form, such as his chairs with the shield-shaped backs. Excellent chairs were made by Thomas Sheraton, with straight legs, turned, fluted, or enriched with delicate carving, or an inlay of coloured woods, and having a delightful reticence of form and treatment.

Early Gothic tables were of the trestle form, the ends being of two pieces, connected by the upper frame and a lower stretcher. The Renascence table retained this form (figs. 1, 2, 4, and 5), which was but a survival of the Greek and Roman marble table (fig. 3). The Elizabethan table had legs of a bulbous form, gadrooned or carved, with upper and lower rails. The Gate-leg table, with spiral or turned legs, is characteristic of the second half of the 17th century. Chippendale frequently used the straight legs and carved or open rails, with a raised fret-work edge round the edge of the table. Side open tables of the late 18th century were frequently inlaid with different coloured woods, or of satin-wood veneer, painted with flowers or wreaths.

Early cupboards were of oak, with pierced and carved tracery panels, which were followed by the linen-fold panel, a favourite mode of enrichment from 1480 to 1560. In the early Renascence (plate 31), the Gothic and classic styles were intermingled, but a little later the panels were carved with medallion-heads and wreaths. This was followed by the classic furniture designed by the French architects Philibert de l'Orme and Du Cerceau, who published a book on

(1) LOUIS XIV. TABLE, MARQUETRY OF BRASS AND TORTOISHELL, WITH ORMOLU MOUNTS;
PROBABLY BY BÉRAIN. (2) LOUIS XV. COMMODE BY JACQUES CAFFIERI, WALLACE
COLLECTION. (3) LOUIS XVI. SIDE TABLE BY J. F. SELEN; PAINTINGS ON GLASS BY
DEGAULT.

furniture in 1550 (fig. 2), and the famous master *ébénistes* of the Renascence, of whom the best known is André Boulle, who used a fine inlay of tortoise-shell and brass ("Boulle work"), also ebony, enhanced with gilded bronze mounts.

In Louis XV.'s reign, Charles Cressent (1685-1768), produced fine examples of furniture with *appliqué ormolu* enrichments. Another great craftsman of this period was Jacques Caffieri, an artist of extraordinary dexterity and caprice in metal mountings for furniture, as may be seen in plate 69 (2). Some beautiful furniture was lacquered with a transparent Vernis Martin.

CONSOLE TABLE CARVED & GILT: PERIOD OF LOUIS SEIZE: 1774-89. S K M.

With Louis XVI. and Marie Antoinette, a reaction set in for more restraint in ornament and severity of line and form, and the beautiful cabinets by Reisener, David Roentgen, and Weisweiter were remarkable for refined craftsmanship and beauty of ornamentation, with a marquetry of flowers, festoons, and diaper borders of rosewood, tulip, pear, and lime upon mahogany and ebony; they were enhanced with bronze mountings by Gouthière, who was a renowned and skilful craftsman.

The Elizabethan and Jacobean periods were famous for their tester bedsteads, which have richly-carved panelled or arcaded backs, the tester also having elaborate panelling and carving. The baluster pillars at the foot usually have square bases, with pierced or open arcadings, and the slender pillars above have wide bulbous divisions, gadrooned or carved.

In Italy, during the 16th century, many beautiful *cassone*, or chests, were produced, enriched with carving (fig. 6), gesso, and gilding, or painted by the great masters of the Renascence. Intarsia (an inlay of wood) was practised in Italy for the enrichment of the beautiful choir stalls, etc., of the 15th and 16th centuries.

SOFA OF CLASSICAL TYPE, BY THOMAS HOPE, *circa* 1800.

CARVED FRAME IN WALNUT, BY ANTONIO BARILI. Late 15ᵗʰ Century. SIENA.

1

2

CENTRE of CARVED TRIPTYCH by VEIT STOSS. SOUTH KENSINGTON MUSEUM.

3

A MISERERE, WESTMINSTER ABBEY.

4

CARVED MIRROR FRAME, GRINLING GIBBONS, 1648-1721. SOUTH KENSINGTON MUSEUM.

5

CARVED AND GILT WOOD PEDESTAL FOR A CANDELABRUM OR "GUERIDON". PERIOD OF LOUIS XIV. S.K.M.

(1) AND (2) PANELS FROM THE CHOIR-STALLS, S. PIETRO, PERUGIA.

(3) AND (4) CHOIR-STALL PANELS, PERUGIA: (3) FROM S. PIETRO, (4) FROM
THE COLLEGIO DEL CAMBIO.

CARVED FRIEZE FROM THE ALTAR, S. MARTINO MAGGIORE, BOLOGNA.

WOOD CARVING.

Wood carving is perhaps one of the earliest and most universal of the industrial arts. The splendid carved statues and statuettes found in the early tombs of Egypt, the vigorous reliefs of the spiral and dragon from the Scandinavian churches (plate 18), the intricate spirals of New Zealand (plate 3), the pierced and carved screens of India, the beautiful carving on the furniture of the Renascence (plate 68), and the delicate and skilful work of Grinling Gibbons (plate 70 (4)) bear tribute to the universal skill of craftsmanship, which reached its highest point of excellence in the later Gothic and Renascence period.

The choir stalls of Amiens Cathedral (plate 25) by Arnold Boulin, Alexander Huet, and Jean Turpin (1508-22), are magnificent examples of the versatility and skill of the flamboyant carver. But France was not alone in the excellence of this craft, for almost contemporaneous are the beautiful doors of the Stanza della Incendio and the Stanza della Eliodoro in the Vatican at Rome (see page 65), by Giovanni Barili, and the choir stalls in S. Pietro, Perugia (plate 71), and in the Cathedral at Siena by Antonio and Giovanni Barili. The magnificent candelabra and the delicate carvings and intarsia in the choir of Santa Marie in Organo, at Verona, by Fra Giovanni da Verona, and the stalls and screen in Santa Maggiore, Bergamo, by Stephano da Bergamo, are some of the finest examples of wood carving in Italy. The richly carved oak stalls by Jörg Syrlin (1464-74) in the Cathedral at Ulm, indicate the beginning of the intricate and florid scroll-work, which became the type of the later German Renascence. The hanging screen and crucifix of S. Lawrence, and the crucifix at S. Sebald's, at Nuremberg (1518), by Veit Stoss (plate 70, fig. 2), are admirable examples of the skilful and florid carving of the German school during the early part of the 16th century.

In Flanders, the splendid chimney-piece in the Palais de Justice, Bruges, with carvings of Charles V. and his ancestors, by Guyot de Beaugrant, from designs by Blondell (1529-31), is rich, yet restrained in treatment, but in the pulpit of the Cathedral at Brussels, by Verbrüggen (1699), carved with figures and foliage, representing the expulsion from Paradise, and in the pulpit by Van de Voort in the Cathedral of Antwerp, carved with naturalistic birds, trees, and figures, extraordinary technical skill is attained, but with a loss of dignity and appropriateness of treatment.

Admirable examples, good in design and technique, abound in English cathedrals, in the screens, canopies, and misereres of the choir stalls (plates 23, 24, 40) of the 14th and 15th centuries, and later.

With Grinling Gibbons wood carving reached its culmination in delicacy and skilful craftsmanship, though too naturalistic and imitative in design (plate 70, fig. 4). His principal works, consisting of flowers, festoons, and birds, are carved chiefly in lime; fine examples are at Belton House and Petworth; and in collaboration with Sir Christopher Wren he executed splendid carvings in the library at Trinity College, Cambridge; S. Paul's Cathedral; S. James's, Piccadilly; the vestry of S. Lawrence, Jewry; and at Hampton Court Palace. Much work attributed to him is, however, by other hands.

FIG 1

TRIPTYCH. FRENCH. 14TH CENTURY
SOUTH KENSINGTON MUSEUM.

2

ASSYRIAN PANEL WITH INCISED
ORNAMENT. BRITISH MUSEUM.

3

TANKARD & COVER. IVORY BODY
IN HIGH RELIEF. ITALIAN 16TH CENTURY.

4

HEAD OF A PASTORAL
STAFF. FRENCH. 14TH CENT.
SOUTH KENSINGTON
MUSEUM.

5

TOP OF MIRROR CASE THE ELOPEMENT OF QUEEN
GUINEVER & SIR LAUNCELOT. FRENCH 14TH CENTURY
SOUTH KENSINGTON MUSEUM.

6

CENTRE OF BOOK COVER
BYZANTINE. 6TH CENTURY
IN MILAN CATHEDRAL.

7

SVMMACHORVM

8

ONE LEAF OF A ROMAN DIPTYCH. 3RD CENTURY
SOUTH KENSINGTON MUSEUM.
THE COMPANION LEAF IN THE CLUNY MUSEUM.

BYZANTINE DIPTYCH. 4TH CENT.
BRITISH MUSEUM.
THE LARGEST KNOWN
IVORY PLAQUE.

9

VIRI. COM. DOMEST EQVIT
ETCONS ORD

LEAF OF
A CONSULAR
DIPTYCH.
OF THE CONSUL ANASTASIUS.
BYZANTINE. 6TH CENTURY.
SOUTH KENSINGTON MUSEUM.

10

HANDLE OF KNIFE

FORK FROM
NURNBERG
MUSEUM
17 CENTURY.

IVORIES.

Doubtless owing to the beautiful texture, colour and adaptability for delicate carving, Ivory has been in use from a remote period. Egypt, Assyria, and India have each contributed many beautiful examples of fine craftsmanship, indicative of the artistic culture of the centuries preceding the Christian Era.

In the Periclean age of Greece, ivory was used for the figure of Athene Parthenos by Pheidias, placed inside the Parthenon. This statue of the standing goddess, 40 ft. high, was of gold and ivory (called *chryselephantine sculpture*), the drapery being of beaten gold and the exposed parts of the figure of carefully-fitted pieces of ivory. A seated *chryselephantine* figure of Jupiter, about 58 ft. high, in the temple of Olympia, was also by Pheidias. Pausanias, the Roman traveller, enumerates some ten *chryselephantine* statues which he saw in his travels (A.D. 140).

The Roman period is noted for the many beautiful Consular diptychs, which may now be seen in our national museums. They consist of two ivory leaves usually 12 by 5 in., the inside having a slightly sunk plane covered with wax for writing upon, the outside being enriched with delicate carved reliefs (figs. 7, 8, and 9). These diptychs were given by new consuls on their appointment, to their friends and officers of the state. The consul is usually represented seated on the cushioned curule chair, or chair of state, and his name is generally written across the top of one leaf.

The Byzantines enriched the covers of their manuscripts with ivory, of which an illustration is given in fig. 6; the ivory throne of Maximian, Archbishop of Ravenna (A.D. 546-556), is also of this period. A beautiful treatment of ivory was used in the 13th and 14th centuries by the Saracens of Egypt; they frequently worked a fine geometric inlay of ivory upon ebony; in other examples ivory panels were pentagonal, hexagonal, or star-shaped, and carved with delicate arabesques, the framing of the panels being of cedar or ebony. In India ivory carving reached a high degree of perfection, especially in the many ivory combs, with pierced and relief work representing the figure of Buddha surrounded with foliage and richly caparisoned elephants.

In the Carlovingian period, 8th to 10th centuries, ivory was largely used for coffers or small chests. During the early Gothic period in Italy and France, ivory crucifixes, pastoral staffs, croziers, statuettes, and triptychs were made in large numbers; and the ivory combs and mirror cases of the Renascence period have fine reliefs of legendary or allegorical subjects. Of pictorial ivories the modern Japanese craftsmen show the highest technical skill, combined with a keen perception of nature and movement, yet their ivories lack the beauty and dignity of composition and the decorative treatment of the early and mediæval ivories.

1. IVORY BOOK COVER. IX CENTURY NORTH ITALY

2. PORTION OF A DURHAM BINDING IN BROWN LEATHER. BENEDICTINE MONASTERY, DURHAM.

3. STAMPED PANEL BY JEHAN NORINS. 1528.

4. STAMPED LEATHER BINDING. "S.T GEORGE" BY JOHN REYNES. 1520. ENGLISH

5. RED MOROCCO BINDING WITH GOLD TOOLING. THO MAIOLI ET AMICOR. BOUND FOR TOMMASO MAIOLI

6. BINDING IN YELLOW MOROCCO TOOLED IN GOLD. GROLIER BINDING.

7. RED MOROCCO BINDING. TOOLED IN GOLD BY NICHOLAS EVE.

8. RED MOROCCO BINDING. TOOLED WITH THE ARMS & CYPHER OF LOUIS XIII

9. PORTION OF BLUE MOROCCO. BINDING BOUND AND TOOLED IN GOLD BY ROGER PAYNE. 1795

OOKBINDINGS.

The covers used to protect manuscripts and printed books have always offered a suitable field for decoration, hence ornamental covers of various periods and materials are numerous. Ivory carved in relief or cut in open work, was frequently used for early Byzantine MSS. (fig. 1). The chief material in use since the 10th century is leather, stamped with dies or tools. An early example dating from the 10th century is of red leather, with a raised interlacing Celtic design, and is now at Stonyhurst. Four remarkable leather bindings were executed at Durham for Bishop Pudsey (1153-95), stamped with small dies, of which there are over 50 varieties. Contemporaneous with these were similar stamped covers of the Winchester Domesday Book, produced at Winchester, and the Liber Sapientiae, at London. The tradition was continued in the 15th century at Oxford, and by Caxton (1477-91), who frequently used intersecting diagonal lines, between which small dies were placed. In the Low Countries and in Germany many beautiful bindings were produced by the panel stamp. The earliest English example has the Arms of Edward IV. impressed. Other fine examples are by F. Egmondt (1493), Richard Pynson (1520), and Jean Norris (1528), who used the acorn panel (fig. 3), and the S. George by John Reynes (fig. 4), who was binder with Thomas Berthelet (1542) to Henry VIII. The introduction of the *roll* in 1530 superseded the panel, and with the exception of those by Nicholas Spering, of Cambridge, these designs with Renascence figures and arcades are not to be compared for vitality and beauty of detail with those of the earlier period.

The gold tooling, which superseded the " blind tooling," was introduced from Saracenic sources into Europe at Venice, where, in 1488, Aldus Manutius commenced his fine series of printed books, and his early bindings (1500-10) had parallel lines and slight Arabic enrichments at the corners. Then followed the beautiful interlacing patterns that were executed for the famous book collectors, Tommaso Maioli and Count Grolier (figs. 5, 6). The Royal bindings for Francois I. and Henry II. were by Peter Roffet, Philip le Noir, and Geoffrey Tory, who probably was also responsible for the Grolier bindings. The 17th century famous French binders were Nicholas and Clovis Eve (fig. 7), Macé Ruette, and Le Gascon, famous for his *pointillé* work. The 18th century binders were N. Boyet, and A. Padeloup, and the Deromes, while the bindings of red morocco with broad tooled borders, executed for the Earl of Oxford (1710-41), known as the Harleian style, and the beautiful and refined bindings by Roger Payne (1795, fig. 9) are of contemporary English work.

The early Grolier tools were distinctly Arabian and solid or barred, while the bindings of " Eve " have interlacing circular and square panels with sprays of foliage. Some French bindings for Henry IV. are tooled with a *semis* of monograms on flowers.

Examples 5 to 9 are in the John Rylands Library, Manchester.

ENGRAVED & PRINTED ORNAMENT.

The earliest printed Books of Hours, of the later 15th and early 16th centuries, retained in a large measure the borders, storiated initials, and allied page ornaments of their illuminated MSS. prototypes. Towards the same period the engraved tokens—often highly decorative—of printers and publishers appear on the title-pages or at the close of books. Slightly later, woodcut or copper-plate head or tail-pieces come into vogue. We are however, less concerned with work of type than with the drawings and engravings of pure ornament freely published from the 16th century onward. These are often explicitly designed for the use of jewellers, architects, intarsia workers, etc., but are none the less adaptable to a variety of crafts. Many noted artists and engravers from Holbein downwards were not above executing such designs singly or in a series. One of the most

JEWELLERY ORNAMENTED BY COLLAERT (16TH CENTURY).

FROM A BOOK OF HOURS. (T. KERVER, PARIS, 1505.)

curious examples, resembling rather an elementary drawing-book, was published in 1540 by Heinrich Vogtherr. More noteworthy executants in the 16th century are Aldegrever, H. S. Beham, Androuet du Cerceau the elder, Etienne de Laune, Woeriot, Flötner, Daniel Mignot, Hans Mielick, Virgil Solis, and Vredeman de Vries. In the 17th century we may

DESIGNS FOR SILVERSMITHS BY PIERRE BOURDON, PARIS (LATE 17TH CENTURY).

note Pierre Le Pautre, Le Brun, Jean Marot, and Simon Gribelin.[1]

[1] This artist, French by origin (b. 1662, d. in London, 1733), produced a book of ornament (published 1682, revised 1710) and an album of Cyphers published in 1697. He designed the

(2) THREE ORNAMENTAL PANELS BY LE PAUTRE, FRENCH, LATE 17TH CENTURY.

(1) FROM SIMON GRIBELIN'S "NEW BOOK OF ORNAMENT," 1710.

The Louis XIV. style finds its principal exponents in Jean Le Pautre, Berain, Daniel Marot, Durant, Bourgnet; and that of Louis XV. in

TWO DESIGNS FROM SIMON GRIBELIN'S "BOOK OF ORNAMENTS," 1682.

Ranson, Meissonnier, Watteau, François Boucher and Pillement; while Salembier, Cauvet, Delafosse, Choffart, Neufforge, Eisen and de Fontanien represent the Louis XVI. period, and Percier and Fontaine the "Empire."

This engraved ornament of the three Renaissance centuries covers a very wide field, and comprises a number of manners and styles. In addition to the numerous pattern books which present designs for jewellers, watch and clock-makers, etc., there are series which claim to be prepared for printers, decorators, carvers, and for the stocks and barrels of guns, etc. There are panels and arabesques, friezes, ceilings, altars, little engraved flowers, and many other motives. Often these are of remarkable delicacy and minuteness, though sometimes meretricious, coarse, clumsy, or grotesque. The above names represent the chief innovators or exponents of their contemporary tastes. The Victoria and Albert Museum is very rich in ornamental pattern-books, covering the whole range of periods and styles.

DESIGN FOR AN ORNAMENTAL PANEL FROM HEILIGENTHAL'S CATALOGUE OF ORNAMENT, STUTTGART, 1832.

book-plate for Worcester College, Oxford, and worked mainly in England. His detail is worked out very minutely, with a feeling for delicacy and proportion, and would look well in jeweller's chasing

157

EGYPTIAN FABRICS.
FROM AKHMIM. 5TH & 6TH CENTURY.
MANCHESTER COLLECTION.

EGYPTIAN FABRIC FROM AKHMIM
6TH CENTURY.
SOUTH KENSINGTON MUSEUM.

SICILIAN 13TH CENTURY. S.K.M.

SOUTH ITALIAN. 14TH CENTURY. S.K.M.

SICILIAN. 13TH CENTURY. S.K.M.

SILK DAMASK. SICILIAN. 13TH CENTURY
SOUTH KENSINGTON MUSEUM.

SICILIAN. 13TH CENTURY.
MANCHESTER COLLECTION

SICILIAN. 13TH CENTURY.
BOCK COLLECTION. MANCHESTER.

VENETIAN. FROM A PERSIAN DESIGN.
15TH CENTURY.

TEXTILE FABRICS.

The utility, universality, construction, texture, ornamentation, and colour of textile fabrics are full of interest and suggestiveness, for in the remarkable development of textile fabrics we may trace the continuity of style and tradition, the intermingling of races and customs, and the grafting of religious ideas with the wealth and luxuriance of the past. All fabrics wrought in the loom are called textiles. They are broadly divided into three classes :— (1) Plain fabrics in which the warp and weft alternate equally ; (2) those fabrics in which a pattern is produced by the warp and weft intermingling in different proportions or colours, figured cloths and tapestries being included in this class ; (3) those fabrics in which the plain textile No. 1 is enriched with the needle, termed embroideries, or by printing, termed printed fabrics.

Owing to their perishable nature, few remains of ancient textile fabrics are in existence. The oldest examples are found in the tombs of Egypt, where, owing to the dryness of the climate, some fabrics of the early dynasties still remain. They are usually of fine linen, and without enrichment, yet upon the same tombs are many painted patterns that undoubtedly show a woven origin. With the exception of a few tapestry fabrics of the XVIII. dynasty, the oldest figured fabrics found in Egypt are of the 6th century A.D., and they show a remarkable similarity to the early patterns of Persia and Byzantium, for it was in India, Persia, and Arabia that textiles reached perfection of workmanship. This splendid tradition was carried from Persia and India to Byzantium in the 5th century, and in the 8th century the Arabians absorbed and assimilated the arts of Persia, India, Egypt, and Spain, and brought the art of weaving to its culmination during the 14th and 15th centuries.

The ornamental designs of textile fabrics of different nations and periods are characterized by well-defined forms, differentiated by racial influence, climatic conditions, and the myths and traditions of the people. Yet the traditional Eastern origin may be traced through many textile designs, for there is no doubt that India, Persia, and Arabia influenced the designs of textile fabrics more than other nations. This was due no doubt partly to the Eastern weavers carrying their art and traditions with them to various parts of Europe, and also to the exportation of their splendid fabrics, but principally to the beautiful and interesting designs, which were perfectly adapted to the process of weaving. It is no doubt this frank adaptation of natural forms and their appropriateness to the technical necessities of woven fabrics, that has rendered this Eastern influence so persistent through many centuries in different parts of Europe. It is remarkable that even in Italy during the whole of the Renascence period, with the characteristic scroll forms and acanthus foliation of its architecture and decorative arts, the textiles are quite distinct in style, having the characteristics of the Sicilian, Persian, and Indian ornament.

In the 12th century, Roger II., the Norman King of Northern Sicily, took Corinth and Argos, and carried many weavers and

SICILIAN FABRIC.

embroiderers from Greece to Sicily, and established them at Palermo, where they quickly assimilated the Sicilian style, and produced many fine fabrics during the 13th and 14th centuries.

The crusades now began to influence the arts. In 1098, Antioch was taken, and the spoil distributed through Europe. In 1204, Constantinople was taken by Baldwin, Count of Flanders, and the Venetian Doge, Dandolo, and the vast spoil of textiles distributed. It was doubtless under the influence of the crusades that the Sicilian weavers of the 13th and 14th centuries produced the many beautiful fabrics enriched with winged lions, foliated crosses and crowns, rayed stars, harts and birds linked together, and with the introduction of armorial bearings. Early in the 14th century this splendid tradition was introduced into Italy, and at Lucca many beautiful fabrics were produced, having the same characteristics and technique as the Sicilian fabrics. The cloak upon the recumbent bronze figure of Richard II., in Westminster Abbey, has a pattern of foliage, with couchant harts and rayed stars, and was most probably copied from the original silk made for Richard at Lucca or Palermo.

The beautiful materials and designs of Indian textile fabrics are indicative of the love of nature and the splendour of colour of a remote antiquity. Though influenced at various times by Greek, Persian, and Arabian traditions, India still preserved an indigenous ornamental art of remarkable freshness and vitality, the designers choosing their own flora and fauna with rare selective power and adaptive qualities. With an instinctive feeling for ornamental art, aided by the splendid colourings of the native dyes, they produced textile fabrics of silks, brocades, and gold and silver lace remarkable for richness and perfection of material, beauty of design, and harmony of colour.

The Indian pine is a familiar form of enrichment, differentiated

161

from the cypress of Persia (fig. 1, plate 48) by the spiral at the apex. This typical pine is treated with a wonderful diversity of detail (figs. 4, 5, and 6, plate 49). The splendid carpets of India were doubtless influenced by the Persian tradition, and they follow the same methods and ornamental arrangements, adapting, conventionalizing, and emphasising plants, flowers, and seeds, and rendering them with a fine feeling for form and colour. Block printing was largely used for silks and cottons, and many splendid examples are now treasured in our museums. An illustration of a printed cotton Palampore from the Victoria and Albert Museum is shown on the previous page, showing the beautiful floral treatment, diversity of detail, and contrast of line and mass. The gold and silver brocades, or " Kincobs," of Ahmedabad and Benares, with patterns of animals, flowers, and foliage richly spangled, the delicate muslins of Dacca, the gold and silver printed muslins of Jaipur, and the woollen shawls of Kashmir with the well-known pine pattern, are splendid examples of richness of material, delicacy and skilfulness of technique, and beauty and appropriateness of ornamentation.

The pile carpets of Persia, especially those of Kurdistan, Khorassan, Kirman, and Ferahan, are the finest in the world, being magnificent in colour and having bold conventional patterns of their beautiful flora, with birds and animals interspersed with the ornament, giving a largeness of mass and interest and vitality of detail. The hyacinth, tulip, iris, and the pink are frequently introduced, together with the hom, or tree of life. An illustration is given (fig. 2, plate 48) of a Genoa fabric, but of Persian design, showing the conventional " pink " with its simplicity and beauty of line. This traditional art of Persia had a most marked influence upon the textile fabrics of Europe from the 12th to the 17th centuries. This was no doubt due to many causes ; but the perfect adaptability to the process of weaving, the interest, inventiveness, and beauty of the ornament, and the singular frank treatment of form and colour, doubtless appealed to the craftsmen of Europe, and hence we find many Persian designs produced in Sicily, Spain, Italy, France, and Flanders.

The finest silk velvets and damasks produced from the looms of Florence show a distinct Persian influence in their bold artichoke and pomegranate patterns. In Genoa, similar patterns in many coloured velvets were produced, and it is singular how largely this persistency of type prevails in all countries.

In 1480, Louis XI. introduced the art into France, when looms were established at Tours, and in 1520 they were established at Lyons by Francois I., and the art of weaving rapidly spread. The earliest fabrics of these looms have patterns similar to the Persian and Italian fabrics ; but soon the vase pattern, which no doubt had its origin in Byzantine textiles and which had been used by the Persians and Italians, began to influence French designs.

However, this rapidly gave place, towards the middle of the 17th century, to the imitation of ribbons and laces in textile fabrics, together with a more naturalistic treatment of floral forms, and the beauty, suggestiveness, and interest of the early patterns now gave way to prettiness, affectation, and a naturalistic treatment which culminated in the period of Madame Pompadour.

The remarkable invention of perforated cards for facilitating the weaving of figured fabrics was introduced by Bonchon (1725), and continued by Falcon in 1728, by Vancanson in 1745, and perfected by Joseph Marie Jacquard in 1804.

The revocation of the Edict of Nantes in 1685 by Louis XIV. caused numbers of weavers to come to England, bringing their art and tradition with them, and many established themselves at Spitalfields. A representative pattern is given in the annexed cut taken from a Spitalfields pattern book now in the Victoria and Albert Museum in which there are many original designs for silk brocades, some by French and others by English designers dating from 1715 to 1754, which was doubtless the most prosperous period of the Spitalfields industry. The patterns, consisting of natural arrangements of flowers, were necessarily largely influenced by fabrics of Lyons.

The textile fabrics of Flanders reached a high degree of perfection in the 16th and 17th centuries, Bruges being famous for its silk damasks and velvets, the patterns showing the traditional Persian, or the pomegranate and artichoke type of the Florentine textiles.

Block printing had been introduced into Flanders in the 15th century, and many fine patterns with Indian motives were produced up to the 17th century.

At Ypres, fine diapered linen was manufactured, and Ghent was famous for its woollens, but the remarkable prosperity of Flanders was destroyed by the Spanish occupation (1556-1648), when large numbers of Flemish weavers came to England and settled in many parts of the country, bringing their traditions and craftsmanship, which have undoubtedly had a most marked influence upon the production of cotton and woollen textile fabrics in England.

Tapestry, of which many fine examples of the 16th and 17th centuries are treasured in our museums and palaces, differs from most

Plate 78.

A DUTCH BOOK END-PAPER OF ABOUT 1800; DESIGN FOUNDED ON
EASTERN STUFFS.

woven fabrics in its method of production, which consists of inter-weaving and knotting short pieces of coloured wefts, which form the pattern, to a strong warp, a ground weft being thrown across each pick to bind the material well together.

This is almost the same method as that used in the manufacture of the Indian and Persian carpets. It was during the 14th and 15th centuries, at Arras in Flanders, that storied tapestries were brought to their culmination, and the tapestry workers became a most power-ful guild. From about 1480, Brussels produced many magnificent hangings from designs by the great masters of the Italian Renascence. Raphael's famous cartoons, which are now in the South Kensington Museum, are the original designs for the ten tapestries manufactured at Brussels for Pope Leo X., for the enrichment of the Sistine Chapel in the Vatican ; the seven cartoons, three being lost, were purchased by Charles I. These cartoons by Raphael were in collaboration with Giovanni da Udine and Francesco Penni, and were in 1515 handed over to the tapestry master, Peter van Aelst, and were completed in 1519.

Many of the great Flemish painters also designed for the Brussels tapestries, such as Van Orley, Van Leyden, and Jan Mabuse.

Francis I. caused tapestry looms to be set up at Fontainebleau in 1539, but it was not until the Gobelin tapestry manufactory was established in 1603 in the Faubourg Saint Marcel by the Fleming, Marc de Comans, and François de la Planche, that French tapestry reached any importance. Under the Minister Colbert in 1667, the Royal Gobelin manufactory produced many fine tapestries designed by the painter, Charles le Brun.

About 1590, some carpets, called Savonnerie, were made in the Louvre, the technique being somewhat similar to the Persian carpets, but the patterns were more pictorial and naturalistic in treatment Fine tapestries were also produced at Beauvais and Aubusson. It was not until the time of James I. that tapestry weaving assumed any importance, when a tapestry manufactory was established (1619) at Mortlake, under the direction of Francis Crane, with skilled weavers from Bruges and Oudenarde, and the master-weaver Philip de Maecht.

In 1662, the painter Antonio Verrio was engaged to supply designs, but owing to a lack of financial support the Mortlake productions ceased in 1700. Other tapestry works were founded at Lambeth, where in 1670 some large tapestries (now in Haddon Hall) were made for the Countess of Rutland.

Some fine Flemish tapestries are in the Victoria and Albert Museum, and eight large pieces by Bernard Van Orley are in the Great Hall of Hampton Court. The coloured cartoons by Mantegna in Hampton Court, representing the triumph of Cæsar, were to be reproduced in tapestry for the Duke of Mantua. There are some fine Gobelin and Beauvais tapestries in Windsor Castle which were gifts from the Court of France, and they all show the most

1. BROCATELLE ITALIAN 16TH CENTURY. S.K.M

2. SINGLE MULLION PATTERN. FLEMISH 16TH CENTURY

3. FLOWER-VASE PATTERN. LATE 16TH CENTURY VENETIAN. BOCK COLLECTION MANCHESTER

4. DOUBLE MULLION PATTERN. ITALIAN 16TH CENTURY. MANCHESTER BOCK COLLECTION

5. VELVET FROM GENOA FROM A PERSIAN DESIGN. 16TH CENTURY. S.K.M

6. VELVET. ITALIAN. 16TH CENTURY MUSÉE DES ARTS DECORATIFS. PARIS

7. SILK. ITALIAN. 16TH CENTURY.

8. SILK BROCADE. 18TH CENTURY.

9. FIGD SATIN. 18TH CENTURY. LYONS.

Plate 80.

JAVANESE FABRICS, 19TH CENTURY.

MANUFACTURED BY THE IKAT PROCESS; A COMBINATION OF WEAVING AND DYEING.

consummate technique, beauty of material, and harmony of colour. The so-called Bayeux tapestry is not tapestry but needlework in coloured wools upon a white linen ground. It is 214 ft. in length and 22 in. in width, and divided into 72 compartments, with incidents representing the Norman invasion of England by William I. Though reputed to be the work of Queen Matilda, the probability is that it is the work of English hands some years after the invasion. This embroidery or tapestry is still preserved in the Cathedral of Bayeux.

The remarkable civilization of the Incas or Peruvians is shown in the many splendid objects of the industrial arts now treasured in our museums. Of these relics of a vanished civilization, the textile fabrics are perhaps the most instructive and interesting. The high technical skill of the craftsmanship, the fine spinning of the wool and cotton, and the perfection of the dyeing of the yarn, together with the skilful weaving of the figured cloths and tapestries, are a tribute to the vitality and civilization of a people remote from all Asiatic or European influences.

These Peruvian textiles are remarkable for the absence of the beautiful flora of Peru as elements for decoration. The fret is a frequent form of enrichment. The wave scroll so typical of Greek work is also a remarkable element in Peruvian ornament, and illustrates the singular development of the same ideas and aspect of form among people so remote from each other as the Greeks and Peruvians. But the patterns that sharply differentiate Peruvian examples from all other styles are the conventional treatments of figures, birds, fishes, and animals. The llama

TAPESTRY IN WHITE & BROWN.

DOUBLE CLOTH IN BROWN & YELLOW. KEY PATTERN IN BROWN & YELLOW.

is conspicuous in many patterns, but the bird forms are the most remarkable, having many variations of type and treatment.

It is difficult to fix any date for these Peruvian examples, but as it is known that during the reign of Inca Pachacutic (*circa* 1390) the ceramic art was at its best, we may assume that the sister art of weaving reached its perfection about the same period, and continued until the Spanish Conquest in the 16th century. Many of the fabrics are of double cloth, of deep brown and pale straw colour, and show the same colour and pattern on both sides of the cloth. Some of the fabrics are tapestry woven, having short strands of coloured wool inserted into the fabric by the aid of the needle.

EMBROIDERY & LACE.

Needlework ornamentation in textile or other materials goes back to a remote period. Actual fragments of Egyptian decorative stitchwork of the 16th and 15th centuries B.C. are preserved, and its general use in Babylon, Assyria, Persia, and other ancient civilizations, may be inferred from wall-paintings and reliefs. Embroidery was known to the Greeks and Romans and, passing from thence to the Byzantines, became rigidly conventionalized, its richness hardly compensating for its stiff, insensitive treatment. From then onwards, the art of embroidery has flourished, being applied principally to hangings, covers, church vestments and state garments. In the 13th century England was famous for her embroidery (*opus anglicanum*) whose surviving masterpiece is the Syon cope at the Victoria and Albert Museum. From the 15th to the 17th centuries embroidery was exceedingly splendid, especially in the varieties known as " black work " and " petit point," the latter often forming elaborate pictures in needlework.

BRIDAL BEDCOVER IN FILET-LACE, FLEMISH, 16TH CENTURY.

LACE, a net-like ornamental openwork of thread (flax, cotton, silk, mohair, gold or silver) is peculiar in that the production of ornament and fabric is simultaneous and inseparable. Its main division is into needlepoint lace and pillow lace. Lace work hardly dates further back than the latter part of the 16th century, the art first attaining perfection in North Italy and Flanders. England borrowed the fashion from France, but for a long time failed to make any state provision for the encouragement of the craft. Among early pattern-books of the 16th and 17th centuries are those of Vinciolo (1587), Vecellio (1592), and Isabetta Parasole. The finest work nowadays is produced in Belgium, France, and the British Isles.

LATE EMPIRE ORNAMENT.

(1) SPANISH AND PORTUGUESE WHITE SATIN DALMATIC,
circa 1600.

(2) SILK HANGING,
ITALIAN, 17TH
CENTURY.

(3) SILK ALTAR FRONTAL, ITALIAN, 17TH CENTURY.

(4) DETAIL OF EMBROIDERY
ON CLOAK, FRENCH,
LATE 16TH OR EARLY
17TH CENTURY.

(a) PAGE FROM A FRENCH BOOK OF HOURS, *circa* 1400.

(b) PAGE FROM A FRENCH BOOK OF HOURS, *circa* 1480.

(c) FROM THE SAME BOOK AS (b). (V. & A.M., SALTING BEQUEST.)

(d) PAGE FROM AN ITALIAN BOOK OF HOURS, *circa* 1520.

ILLUMINATED MSS.

No form of artistic expression is more imbued with the very spirit of the Middle Ages than the illuminated manuscript. Although its origins may be retraced to a remote date—in embryo we find examples among Egyptian papyri and classical MSS.—it is none the less true to describe it in its highest development as a typically mediæval product. An illuminated manuscript usually comprises three elements : *the written text* (often an ornament in itself) ; the *pictures*, or pictorial motives (" histories " as they were termed) ; and the purely decorative *motives* (chiefly borders and large initials). The scribe was invariably distinct from the artist, or artists, we might say, as the pictures and decorative motives were apt to be by different hands, even where the miniatures are the work of a single artist.

In the earlier book of the Byzantine and Frankish periods, richness of effect is often obtained by a background of gold-leaf, or staining with purple, against which pictures, initials, etc., stand out strikingly. The initials to the four gospels are usually treated as full-page ornamental designs, often of great beauty and originality. The decoration of the Celtic MS. of the 7th, 8th, and 9th centuries (*e.g.* the Book of Kells, the Book of Armagh, Lindisfarne Gospels, etc., *cf.* plate 17) are remarkable for their intricate convolutions, largely based on the fret-pattern. Gold is hardly ever used in these, but this is compensated for by brilliancy of colour and design ; animal forms though freely introduced are highly conventionalized and subordinated to the general pattern.

From the 13th to the 15th century there is a steady progression of excellence in the art of illumination in all its branches. The ornamental borders so characteristic of the later period are at first in the nature of ornamental flourishes prolonging the great initials along the margins, which they gradually fill on three, then on all four sides of the text.

In a general way the illuminated MS. may be said to have reached its zenith about 1380-1450. The simple, yet rich and delicate, leaf borders that fill the margins in the earlier part of this period are succeeded by the more pretentious floral designs, relieved with pictorial and animal motives much favoured by the Burgundian school. These again were succeeded by borders of solid brush gold, on which were depicted with scrupulous realism flowers, insects, and fruit (occasionally varied by landscape and architectural borders). The Italians from about 1480 favoured elaborate borders in shaded gold, " camaïeu " and the like, composed of classical columns, urns, shields, acanthus leaves, mascarons, etc., on a ground of crimson or black ; or a characteristic variant of white scroll-work on a blue ground dotted with white. The latest borders are commonly wholly pictorial in treatment ; in other words, the miniature forms a frame for the text.

But from *c.* 1480 the decline is clearly marked, and despite some brilliant exceptions, the art may be considered as dead towards the middle of the 16th century.

Perhaps the highest achievement of the art of illumination is the " Très Riches Heures," once belonging to John, Duke of Berry, and now at Chantilly. Among names of famous miniaturists known to us are : Hubert Van Eyck,[1] Pol de Limburg, and his brothers, Jehan and François Fouquet, Philip de Mazerolles, Simon Marmion, Jean Bourdichon, Gerard of Bruges, Memling, and Simon Bening.

The commonest (and often richest) MSS. were those described as *liturgical*, including antiphonars, bibles, books of hours, breviaries, gospels, graduals, missals, and psalters. The books of hours (intended for private devotion) outnumber the rest by perhaps 10 to 1.

[1] To whom Durrien and Hulin de Lou independently ascribe the exquisite " Heures de Turin," unfortunately burnt in 1904.

ILLUMINATED PAGE FROM FRENCH GOSPELS, LATE 14TH CENTURY.

(1) CANVAS CUSHION COVER EMBROIDERED IN COLOURED SILKS. 18TH CENT. CRETAN EMBROIDERY (V. & A.M.).
(2) EMBOSSED LEATHER POUCH, NORTH GERMANY. A.D. 1739.

(3) APPLIQUÉ AND EMBROIDERED LEATHER BELTS, LINZ, UPPER AUSTRIA.

PEASANT ART.

Although characteristic examples of peasant art are to be seen in many museums, in this country, at least, we seem to have no collection of such productions arranged according to district of origin. The productions of the peasantry often vary not only from province to province, but from village to village, and are, generally speaking, influenced by conventions akin to those that obtain in more primitive cultures : *e.g.* the carved wood is not entirely dissimilar to that of Oceania (*cf.* plate 3). These arts are usually characterised by a charming, if sometimes rather casual, naïveté, and often by a native sense of design and colour-distribution. The peasant art of the Balkan States and neighbouring countries is thought to have been materially affected by Oriental influences, whilst the folk embroideries of Spain are reputed to be worked in a technique handed down from the Moors.

These handicrafts flourished most vigorously in the 17th and 18th centuries, but the work was often continued into the 19th century, and is only now actually dying out. There are important schools in Russia, Germany, Scandinavia, Switzerland, the Tyrol, Austria, and Hungary. The Central European countries produce elaborate fretted carvings often applied to furniture and exteriors ; Norway makes carved and gaily painted wooden objects similar to those of the Tyrol ; Germany has distinctive local types in Swabia, Brandenburg, Bavaria, etc., and Czecho-Slovakia is remarkable for embroideries, as are also the Dalmatian districts. In this the design is often highly conventionalized with use of traditional abstract forms (plate 83).

England cannot show much art of this type, but mention should be made of the Sussex ironwork industry which produced wrought or cast firebacks, potcranes, etc. ; of the old samplers and smocks, and the lace of Devonshire and North Buckinghamshire ; the flourishing Buckinghamshire chair-turning, which is more a traditional handicraft than an art.

The rise of modern mechanical mass-production, and improved communications have naturally succeeded in almost obliterating these small native arts and handicrafts, and it would be well if some full museum collection could be made of them, whilst still in existence, to form an epitome of the fresh and instinctive peasant work of the last few centuries.

TRADITIONAL CUT PAPER DESIGNS.

GREEK FRET
RIGHT-ANGLED & UNIFORM

GREEK FRET
RIGHT-ANGLED

MORESQUE FRET
RIGHT-ANGLED LINES
COMBINED WITH DIAGONALS

JAPANESE
OBLONG FRET.
RIGHT-ANGLED LINES

BYZANTINE FRET
COMBINATION OF CURVED & STRAIGHT LINES.
A PIERCED MARBLE PANEL FROM THE
CHURCH OF S APOLLINARE RAVENNA

JAPANESE FRET DIAPER

JAPANESE.
DISCONNECTED
FRET

MORESQUE FRET.
RIGHT-ANGLED & DIAGONAL LINES

ASSYRIAN GUILLOCHE.

EGYPTIAN CURVED FRET

GREEK WAVE

BYZANTINE GUILLOCHE.

CELTIC FRET.
RIGHT-ANGLED & DIAGONAL
LINES CUT WITH CURVED
ANGLES.

FRETS.

The remarkable universality of the fret, the simplicity and rhythm of detail, its adaptability and usefulness for surface enrichment, have made the fret one of the best known forms of ornamentation. It was used in the surface decorations of the tombs of Egypt, the temples of Greece, and the civic and domestic buildings of Rome.

The Greek form with its right-angular and equally-spaced keys, was used on the simple abacus and plain fascias of the Dorian architecture, in bands upon the painted vases, and in a concentric form when used in the interior of the red-figured circular cylix. The Romans, without imparting freshness used the same right-angled key-pattern, chiefly as borders for mosaic pavements and upon the horizontal soffits of their architecture. The Byzantine, using the same type in conjunction with the cross and circle, gave more significance to the fret.

The Arabian fret differs in the use of the oblique line, together with the right-angled key, obtaining a wonderful degree of complexity and richness.

The Celtic fret is chiefly a diagonal one, but the recurrent angle is rounded to a curve.

Chinese and Japanese frets are usually right-angled, and are used in great profusion, often in a secondary field or background.

The Japanese key or "*Fret diaper*" is used in the greatest profusion; it is used alike on silks and brocades, damascened

WALL-MOSAIC OF COLOURED MARBLES

in metal, in cloisonné enamel and in lacquered work, and is frequently arranged in irregular shaped compartments or medallions.

The Greek continuous fret border is rarely used by the Japanese,

who generally use the disconnected or irregular fret. A similar irregular fret border was used by the Peruvians (pages 115 and 167), by the Mexicans, and by the natives of Polynesia.

The Assyrian and Byzantine guilloche is but a curved fret, but additional interest is given by the introduction of radiating forms in the principal interstices of the fret.

The simplest form of construction for frets, or key patterns, is to use squared or ruled paper. The Chinese or Japanese key is comparatively simple to construct by making the double T 17 squares in length with arms at each end of 13 squares, and placed alternately at right angles to each other.

PRINTED INITIAL LETTERS.

The initial letter, with its beauty of line and colour, its emphasis and distinctive character, was a frequent form of enrichment to the beautiful early manuscripts, and when, in the latter part of the 15th century, the printed book began to supersede the MS., the "Illuminator," or rubricator, was still called upon to enrich the printed page with his beautiful initials. Frequently, however, the rubricator was not called upon, with the result that many of the early printed books are still without their intended initial letters, as we find in many of the magnificent folios issued from the Aldine Press at Venice about 1500.

When the printed initial first made its appearance, it necessarily followed the type and character of the illuminated examples, as in the fine B (page 33), from the Mainz Psalter [1] in red and black, which is the earliest example known printed with the text (1457), and this initial is distinctly based upon the earlier illuminated capital.

Illustrations are given on pages 7, 9, 11, 23, 89, 105, 119, 147 of eight beautiful printed initials from the "Suetonius" of 1470 [1] by the Germans, Conrad Sweynheim and Arnold Pannartz, who in 1456 introduced the art of printing into Italy at the Benedictine Monastery at Subiaco, near Rome. These initials, with their distinctive and refined Roman type, and delicate interlacing scrolls, are admirable examples of the early printed initial. They were afterwards acquired by Riessinger, who used them in 1480-98 for his printed books at Rome. The examples, with well-designed interlacings, given on pages 37, 39, 103, and those on 55 and 81 are taken from the fine "Euclid" by Ratdolt, of Venice, printed in 1481.[1] Three excellent initials from the beautiful printed books by Aldus Manutius, at Venice,[1] are given on pages 7, 95, 125.

Well-designed Gothic initials are given on page 15 from the "Fasciculus Temporum" (1481) by Ratdolt of Venice, the D (page 51) by Antonios Campigollis (1475), and the N from the "Life of Campanus," by M. Feronis, at Milan (1495, page 40). Beautiful Gothic initials given on pages 27, 137, 151, 159, 173, having well-spaced conventional foliage and flowers, are taken from "Froissart's Cronycles," printed in London by Richard Pynson (1523).[1] Other examples are the two from the Golden Bible (pages 35, 103) and the C on page 109 from the "Missale Traijectense" (1515), showing an intricate interlacing of the letter itself, the same characteristic appearing in the Romaunt of the Rose given on pages 73, 123, 129, 155.

Two rich examples of foliated initials by Israel van Meckenen (1500) are given on pages 58 and 87. The P on page 31 is from Venice (1498) ; the N, page 47, is dated 1510 ; the G, page 133, is from the Flemish woodcut alphabet of 1464 (British Museum) ; and the T on page 175 is from the Basle woodcut copy of this alphabet.

The Italian examples on pages 139 and 174 illustrate the decorative use of the figure in the early 16th-century initials.

[1] From the original editions in the John Rylands Library.

ERMS USED IN ORNAMENTAL ART.

Ornament is the means by which Beauty or Significance is imparted to Utility. It is either Symbolical or Æsthetic. Symbolic ornament consists of elements or forms chosen for the sake of their *significance*—Æsthetic ornament consists of forms or elements chosen for their *beauty* alone, or their power of appealing to the senses.

Of the historic styles of ornament, the Egyptian, Assyrian, Byzantine, Scandinavian, Persian, Indian, Gothic, Polynesian, and much of the Chinese and Japanese are symbolical, having elements and ornamental details chosen for their significance; while in the Greek, Roman, and Renascence ornament the purely æsthetic motive is characteristic.

Ornament, again, may be natural or conventional—Imitative or Inventive. The terms "natural" and "imitative" have the same significance—viz., the exact copying of natural forms, so that they become principal, not secondary as perfect ornament should be. Conventional ornament is the adaptation of natural forms to ornamental and technical requirements, and is seen in its greatest beauty in the frank treatment by the Indians and Persians of their flora and fauna for the decorative enrichment of their textile fabrics, pottery, and jewellery.

Inventive ornament is that which consists of elementst no derived from any natural source; the Moresque style is a good example of this type.

The *elements* of ornament are the details or forms chosen for ornamental motives, and the *principles* of ornament are the arrangement of these forms and details; they comprise repetition, alternation, symmetry, radiation, balance, proportion, variety, eurythmy, contrast, intersection, complication, fitness, and utility.

Repetition is the use of elements in a continuous series; *Alternation* is the repetition of an element at intervals, with others intervening; *Symmetry :* when the leading lines are equal or similar (or reciprocal) on both sides; *Radiation :* when the lines spring from a centre, for example, a bird's wing and the flower of the daisy; *Balance* and *Proportion :* when the relation and harmony of parts is based upon natural laws; *Variety* implies difference in the details, with respect to form or type; *Eurythmy* signifies rhythms or harmony in ornament; *Contrast* is the arrangement in close proximity of colours or forms of opposite characters, as the straight line with the curve, or light with dark; *Intersection* is the crossing of the leading lines, the Arabian, Moresque and Celtic styles are examples of this principle; *Complication* is the effect produced by elements so arranged as to be more or less difficult to trace with the eye alone: as in the Japanese key and the Moresque star pattern. *Fitness* and *utility* as their names imply are essentials in all good periods of ornamentation.

175

INDEX.